Quick Fix

for Bible junkies

Benjamin Ward

CrossBooks™
A Division of LifeWay
1663 Liberty Drive
Bloomington, IN 47403
www.crossbooks.com
Phone: 1-866-879-0502

First published by CrossBooks 04/06/2010

ISBN: 978-1-6150-7161-6 (sc)
Library of Congress Control Number: 2010923659

Printed in the United States of America
Bloomington, Indiana

This book is printed on acid-free paper.

Dedication:

This is for you.

Special Thanks to
My family and friends for giving me
the support I needed to complete the task at hand.
And
www.quickfixforbiblejunkies.com
for connecting me to the world.

TABLE OF CONTENTS

Why Junkie Why?

Bible junkie - Bi·ble junk·y
1. a Bible addict
2. somebody whose interest in or liking for biblical wisdom and understanding resembles an addiction (informal)

Knowing Christ's lordship over me took me to many places I thought I'd never go. I realized something in Laos I wasn't hungry for the Bible. I thought if I didn't know something in the Bible, it was okay. After all, I loved God as His child. Not understanding Him was not a problem. Ignorance was a part of my role as His creation.

In truth, I ignored the gift of God's Word, because I didn't enjoy reading it. I'm dyslexic, and reading has never been easy for me. I'd rather pray or worship.

One day, while praying, it struck me. My neglect to pay attention to and meditate in the Word was hurting my relationship with the Lord. I asked Jesus to change this in me. He did. Isolating me from the other Christians, He gave me a new craving for His Word. I began to write my thoughts on the passages He drew me to read. Over my six-month in Asia, I did an in-depth study of four books, which took me hundreds of hours.

This time with the Lord gave me a new intimacy with Him. I realized I was craving the Word. It was more than a mere hunger; I had become an addict. If I did not study and get my fix of the Word, I did not feel right. What a great answer to my prayer.

Reading the Bible still wasn't easy for me, and I realized that others might have the same problem. So, here's the *Quick Fix for Bible Junkies*!

This book is for you Bible junkies and all those who hope to be one someday. I made the fixes short enough for you to read, think about, and let them sink in. I used five different Bible translations in this book. Those capital letters after the numbers stand for which Bible I'm quoting, but each one is God's Word.

God's not far away. He can speak to us when we aren't too distracted to hear. When God gives you something, write it down.

Psalm 107:9(NKJV)

"For He satisfies the longing soul, And fills the hungry soul with goodness."

Luke 1:53(NIV)

"He has filled the hungry with good things but has sent the rich away empty."

Fixes Everyone Needs to Know:

These fixes are basics.

Luke 1:37(WEB)

"For with God nothing will be impossible."

Jeremiah 32:17(NASB)

"Ah Lord GOD! Behold, You have made the heavens and the earth by Your great power and by Your outstretched arm! Nothing is too difficult for You."

Romans 4:21(NLT)

"He was absolutely convinced that God was able to do anything he promised."

Junkie Fix

God is big and powerful enough to do *anything.*

MARK 12:27(NKJV)

"He is not the God of the dead, but the God of the living. You are therefore greatly mistaken."

Junkie Fix

He is the way to eternal life.

Romans 3:23(WEB)

"For all have sinned, and come short of the glory of God; Being justified freely by his grace, through the redemption that is in Jesus Christ."

Ephesians 1:7(NKJV)

"In Him we have redemption through His blood, the forgiveness of sins, according to the riches of His grace."

Ephesians 2:8(NASB)

"For by grace you have been saved through faith; and that not of yourselves, it is the gift of God."

Junkie Fix

No one deserves forgiveness. It is His gift of His grace.

MARK 13:31(NKJV)

"Heaven and earth will pass away, but My words will by no means pass away."

ISAIAH 40:8(NKJV)

"The grass withers, the flower fades, but the word of our God stands forever."

2 PETER 3:7(NASB)

"But by His word, the present heavens and earth are being reserved for fire, kept for the day of judgment and destruction of ungodly men."

....

....

....

....

....

....

....

....

....

....

....

JUNKIE FIX

....

EVERYTHING WILL DISAPPEAR AND PASS AWAY *EXCEPT* THE WORD OF GOD.

Mark 10:27(NIV)

"Jesus looked at them and said, 'With man this is impossible, but not with God; all things are possible with God.'"

Job 42:2(NKJV)

"'I know that You can do everything, and that no purpose of Yours can be withheld from You."

Junkie Fix

God's grace saves me. Not my works. I'm amazed that I can do miraculous things with Christ's authority.

Acts 20:32(WEB)

"And now, brethren, I commend you to God, and to the word of his grace, which is able to build you up, and to give you an inheritance among all them who are sanctified."

Hebrews 9:15(WEB)

"And for this cause he is the mediator of the new testament, that by means of death, for the redemption of the transgressions that were under the first testament, they who are called may receive the promise of eternal inheritance."

....

....

....

....

....

....

....

....

....

....

....

Junkie Fix

....

Jesus is Christ. He is why I will go to heaven.

LUKE 22:19(NKJV)

"And He took bread, gave thanks and broke it, and gave it to them, saying, 'This is My body which is given for you; do this in remembrance of Me.'"

1 PETER 2:24(NKJV)

"Who Himself bore our sins in His own body on the tree, that we, having died to sins, might live for righteousness—by whose stripes you were healed."

JUNKIE FIX

JESUS' SACRIFICE WAS FOR ME. THE PAIN, PERSECUTION, AND REJECTION WERE FOR MY SAKE.

LUKE 15:7(NIV)

"'I tell you that in the same way there will be more rejoicing in heaven over one sinner who repents than over ninety-nine righteous persons who do not need to repent.'"

LUKE 5:32(WEB)

"I came not to call the righteous, but sinners to repentance."

LUKE 15:10(NLT)

"In the same way, there is joy in the presence of God's angels when even one sinner repents."

LUKE 15:24(WEB)

"For this my son was dead, and is alive again; he was lost, and is found. And they began to be merry."

LUKE 19:10(NIV)

"For the Son of Man came to seek and to save what was lost."

1 PETER 2:10(NLT)

"Once you were not a people; now you are the people of God. Once you received none of God's mercy; now you have received his mercy."

Junkie Fix

God came for me, the sinner.

Luke 12:4(NLT)

"Dear friends, don't be afraid of those who want to kill you. They can only kill the body; they cannot do any more to you."

Psalm 119:120(NASB)

"My flesh trembles for fear of You, and I am afraid of Your judgments."

Isaiah 51:7(NLT)

"Listen to me, you who know right from wrong and cherish my law in your hearts. Do not be afraid of people's scorn or their slanderous talk. For the moth will destroy them as it destroys clothing. The worm will eat away at them as it eats wool. But my righteousness will last forever. My salvation will continue from generation to generation."

Isaiah 51:12(NKJV)

"I, even I, am He who comforts you. Who are you that you should be afraid of a man who will die, and of the son of a man who will be made like grass?"

Jeremiah 1:8(NIV)

"'Do not be afraid of them, for I am with you and will rescue you,' declares the Lord."

Luke 12:5(NIV)

"But I will show you whom you should fear Fear him who, after the killing of the body, has power to throw you into hell. Yes, I tell you, fear him."

Junkie Fix

God is greater than any other power. Whom will I serve?

MARK 9:37(NASB)

"Whoever receives one child like this in My name receives Me; and whoever receives Me does not receive Me, but Him who sent Me."

LUKE 10:16(NKJV)

"He who hears you hears Me, he who rejects you rejects Me, and he who rejects Me rejects Him who sent Me."

JUNKIE FIX

BELIEVERS REPRESENT CHRIST, AND CHRIST THE FATHER, SO ALL BLESSINGS WILL BE PASSED ON.

Luke 23:41(NKJV)

"And we indeed justly, for we receive the due reward of our deeds; but this Man has done nothing wrong."

Peter 2:21(NIV)

"To this you were called, because Christ suffered for you, leaving you an example that you should follow in his steps. 'He committed no sin, and no deceit was found in his mouth.' When they hurled their insults at him, he did not retaliate; when he suffered, he made no threats. Instead, he entrusted himself to him who judges justly. He himself bore our sins in his body on the tree, so that we might die to sins and live for righteousness; by his wounds you have been healed. For you were like sheep going astray, but now, you have returned to the Shepherd and Overseer of your souls."

....

....

....

....

....

....

....

....

Junkie Fix

I deserve only evil for my sin. But by grace through sinless Jesus, I am saved. He even restores me to righteousness.

LUKE 24:46(NASB)

"And He said to them, 'Thus it is written, that the Christ would suffer and rise again from the dead the third day, and that repentance for forgiveness of sins would be proclaimed in His name to all the nations, beginning from Jerusalem.'"

ACTS 17:2(NASB)

"And according to Paul's custom, he went to them, and for three Sabbaths reasoned with them from the Scriptures, explaining and giving evidence that the Christ had to suffer and rise again from the dead, and saying, 'This Jesus whom I am proclaiming to you is the Christ.'"

JUNKIE FIX

JESUS HAD TO DIE AND RISE. I HAVE TO TELL OTHERS HE IS CHRIST.

Luke 20:38(NASB)

"Now He is not the God of the dead but of the living; for all live to Him."

Romans 6:10(NASB)

"For the death that He died, He died to sin once for all; but the life that He lives, He lives to God. Even so, consider yourselves to be dead to sin, but alive to God in Christ Jesus."

John 14:6(NLT)

"Jesus told him, 'I am the way, the truth, and the life. No one can come to the Father except through me.'"

Junkie Fix

He is the life. The only way to heaven and an eternity is with Him. Any other path is death.

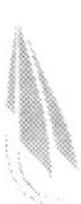

LUKE 13:29(NIV)

"People will come from east and west and north and south, and will take their places at the feast in the kingdom of God."

ISAIAH 66:18(NKJV)

"For I know their works and their thoughts. It shall be that I will gather all nations and tongues; and they shall come and see My glory."

MALACHI 1:11(NIV)

"'My name will be great among the nations, from the rising to the setting of the sun. In every place incense and pure offerings will be brought to my name, because my name will be great among the nations,' says the Lord Almighty."

....

....

....

....

....

....

....

....

JUNKIE FIX

....

PEOPLE FROM ALL THE WORLD WILL BE IN HEAVEN.

LUKE 1:52(NIV)

"He has brought down rulers from their thrones but has lifted up the humble."

1 SAMUEL 2:8(NIV)

"He raises the poor from the dust and lifts the needy from the ash heap; he seats them with princes and has them inherit a throne of honor. For the foundations of the earth are the Lord's; upon them he has set the world."

JUNKIE FIX

GOD IS AMAZING! I AM SUCH A SINNER YET HE CHOOSES TO USE ME.

ACTS 2:38(NASB)

"Peter said to them, 'Repent, and each of you be baptized in the name of Jesus Christ for the forgiveness of your sins; and you will receive the gift of the Holy Spirit.'"

MATTHEW 4:17(NLT)

"From then on, Jesus began to preach, 'Turn from your sins and turn to God, because the Kingdom of Heaven is near.'"

ACTS 3:19(NKJV)

"Repent therefore and be converted, that your sins may be blotted out, so that times of refreshing may come from the presence of the Lord,"

ACTS 5:31(NASB)

"He is the one whom God exalted to His right hand as a Prince and a Savior, to grant repentance to Israel, and forgiveness of sins.

....

....

....

....

JUNKIE FIX

REPENT...IS A LITTLE WORD THAT MEANS EVERYTHING, WHEN IT SINKS IN.

Acts 2:36(NASB)

"Therefore let all the house of Israel know for certain that God has made Him both Lord and Christ—this Jesus whom you crucified."

Acts 2:23(NKJV)

"Him, being delivered by the determined purpose and foreknowledge of God, you have taken by lawless hands, have crucified, and put to death;"

Acts 5:30(NKJV)

"The God of our fathers raised up Jesus whom you murdered by hanging on a tree."

Junkie Fix

Blame no one else for Christ's Crucifixion... He did it for me.

Acts 10:28(NKJV)

"Then he said to them, "You know how unlawful it is for a Jewish man to keep company with or go to one of another nation. But God has shown me that I should not call any man common or unclean.

Acts 15:7(NASB)

"After there had been much debate, Peter stood up and said to them, 'Brethren, you know that in the early days God made a choice among you, that by my mouth the Gentiles would hear the word of the gospel and believe. And God, who knows the heart, testified to them giving them the Holy Spirit, just as He also did to us;'"

Junkie Fix

No difference is so great between me and someone else that I can't share the Word with them.

ACTS 10:34(NIV)

"Then Peter began to speak 'I now realize how true it is that God does not show favoritism but accepts men from every nation who fear him and do what is right. You know the message God sent to the people of Israel, telling the good news of peace through Jesus Christ, who is Lord of all.'"

Junkie Fix

No "out of bounds" exist for Christ.

ACTS 10:42(NKJV)

"And He commanded us to preach to the people, and to testify that it is He who was ordained by God to be Judge of the living and the dead."

MATTHEW 10:27(NIV)

"What I tell you in the dark, speak in the daylight; what is whispered in your ear, proclaim from the roofs. Do not be afraid of those who kill the body but cannot kill the soul. Rather, be afraid of the One who can destroy both soul and body in hell."

JOHN 5:27(NKJV)

"And has given Him authority to execute judgment also, because He is the Son of Man. Do not marvel at this; for the hour is coming in which all who are in the graves will hear His voice and come forth--those who have done good, to the resurrection of life, and those who have done evil, to the resurrection of condemnation."

....

....

....

....

....

JUNKIE FIX

....

THIS IS NOT A GAME. SIN IS DEATH AND ONLY JESUS CAN SAVE US.

Luke 24:27(NKJV)

"And beginning at Moses and all the Prophets, He expounded to them in all the Scriptures the things concerning Himself."

Genesis 12:3(NIV)

"I will bless those who bless you, and whoever curses you I will curse; and all peoples on earth will be blessed through you."

Deuteronomy 18:15(NKJV)

"The Lord your God will raise up for you a Prophet like me from your midst, from your brethren. Him you shall hear,"

Psalm 132:11(NLT)

"The Lord swore to David a promise he will never take back "I will place one of your descendants on your throne."

Isaiah 7:14(NKJV)

"Therefore the Lord Himself will give you a sign Behold, the virgin shall conceive and bear a Son, and shall call His name Immanuel."

Isaiah 9:6(NKJV)

For unto us a Child is born, unto us a Son is given; and the government will be upon His shoulder. And His name will be called Wonderful, Counselor, Mighty God, Everlasting Father, Prince of Peace.

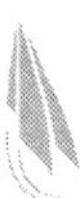

Jeremiah 23:5(NASB)

"'Behold, the days are coming,' declares the Lord, 'When I will raise up for David a righteous Branch; And He will reign as king and act wisely And do justice and righteousness in the land.'"

Daniel 9:24(NLT)

"A period of seventy sets of seven has been decreed for your people and your holy city to put down rebellion, to bring an end to sin, to atone for guilt, to bring in everlasting righteousness, to confirm the prophetic vision, and to anoint the Most Holy Place."

Romans 1:1(NKJV)

"Paul, a bondservant of Jesus Christ, called to be an apostle, separated to the gospel of God which He promised before through His prophets in the Holy Scriptures, concerning His Son Jesus Christ our Lord, who was born of the seed of David according to the flesh, and declared to be the Son of God with power according to the Spirit of holiness, by the resurrection from the dead. Through Him we have received grace and apostleship for obedience to the faith among all nations for His name, among whom you also are the called of Jesus Christ;"

John 5:39(NKJV)

"You search the Scriptures, for in them you think you have eternal life; and these are they which testify of Me."

Junkie Fix

Jesus is the Savior who was foretold would come.

Stop. Let everything I have just meditated on sink in. Over the years, I have learned what it means to be a Christian but every so often, I need to return to the basics to make sure I haven't lost my way.

God is powerful, so powerful He can do anything including using me for His good works. I don't deserve the blessings and salvation He has given me, but it is in His will and it is my gift. I can trust the Bible. It is perfect. It will never be destroyed. I know that God wants me to tell everyone about Christ even when it makes me feel uncomfortable.

God has put me in the lives of many people; some good, some bad, some foolish and others are wicked. I am on Earth to share Christ with each of them. I can't imagine God's heartbreak, knowing that his creations don't know Him, don't love Him, or even worse, don't love Him enough to be uncomfortable for Him. I have been scared, sick, and dying but I live because God gives me life. I serve Him with every breath.

I am not perfect but this book is part of what God asked me to do, share what I have been taught. Share with people I know and love and share with people I don't know or may never meet. I pray that other Christians will stand up and do what God asks, not leaving it for someone else. God made you for a reason.

Spirit Fixes

Holy Spirit and Soul stuff.

LUKE 16:17(NASB)

"But it is easier for heaven and earth to pass away than for one stroke of a letter of the Law to fail."

Psalm 102:26(NKJV)

"They will perish, but You will endure; Yes, they will all grow old like a garment; Like a cloak You will change them, And they will be changed. But You are the same, And Your years will have no end."

Isaiah 40:8(NLT)

"The grass withers, and the flowers fade, but the word of our God stands forever."

Isaiah 51:6(NKJV)

"Lift up your eyes to the heavens, And look on the earth beneath. For the heavens will vanish away like smoke, The earth will grow old like a garment, And those who dwell in it will die in like manner; But My salvation will be forever, And My righteousness will not be abolished."

....

....

....

....

Junkie Fix

Every physical thing will have an end but the spiritual things of God are forever.

ROMANS 5:6(NLT)

"When we were utterly helpless, Christ came at just the right time and died for us sinners.

GALATIANS 2:20(NIV)

"I have been crucified with Christ and I no longer live, but Christ lives in me. The life I live in the body, I live by faith in the Son of God, who loved me and gave himself for me.

EPHESIANS 5:2(NKJV)

"And walk in love, as Christ also has loved us and given Himself for us, an offering and a sacrifice to God for a sweet-smelling aroma."

....

....

....

....

....

....

....

....

....

JUNKIE FIX

....

A GIFT HAS BEEN GIVEN. I ACCEPT IT, KNOWING I DON'T DESERVE IT.

ROMANS 5:9(NASB)

"Much more then, having now been justified by His blood, we shall be saved from the wrath of God through Him."

1 JOHN 1:7(NKJV)

"But if we walk in the light as He is in the light, we have fellowship with one another, and the blood of Jesus Christ His Son cleanses us from all sin."

....

....

....

....

....

....

....

....

....

....

....

....

....

....

JUNKIE FIX

....

CHRIST SAVED ME. NOW I AM BOUND TO HIM.

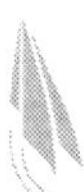

ROMANS 6:14(NLT)

"Sin is no longer your master, for you are no longer subject to the law, which enslaves you to sin. Instead, you are free by God's grace."

EPHESIANS 1:6(NKJV)

"To the praise of the glory of His grace, by which He made us accepted in the Beloved."

2CORINTHIANS 2:9(NIV)

"The reason I wrote to you was to see if you would stand the test and be obedient in everything."

JUNKIE FIX

I AM DAMNED WITHOUT GRACE.

ROMANS 2:13(NASB)

"For it is not the hearers of the Law who are just before God, but the doers of the Law will be justified."

MATTHEW 7:21(NKJV)

"Not everyone who says to Me, 'Lord, Lord,' shall enter the kingdom of heaven, but he who does the will of My Father in heaven."

JAMES 1:25(NIV)

"But the man who looks intently into the perfect law that gives freedom, and continues to do this, not forgetting what he has heard, but doing it—he will be blessed in what he does.

Junkie Fix

Just listening to sermons will not get me into Heaven. I must believe Christ

ROMANS 2:11(NIV)

"For God does not show favoritism."

JOB 34:19(NKJV)

"Yet He is not partial to princes, Nor does He regard the rich more than the poor; For they are all the work of His hands."

EPHESIANS 6:9(NLT)

"And in the same way, you masters must treat your slaves right. Don't threaten them; remember, you both have the same Master in heaven, and he has no favorites."

....

....

....

....

....

....

....

....

....

....

JUNKIE FIX

....

GOD WILL JUDGE ME FAIRLY.

ACTS 13:36(NKJV)

"For David, after he had served his own generation by the will of God, fell asleep, was buried with his fathers, and saw corruption; but He whom God raised up saw no corruption. Therefore let it be known to you, brethren, that through this Man is preached to you the forgiveness of sins;

Jeremiah 31:34(NASB)

"They will not teach again, each man his neighbor and each man his brother, saying, 'Know the Lord, for they will all know Me, from the least of them to the greatest of them,' declares the Lord, 'for I will forgive their iniquity, and their sin I will remember no more.'"

Junkie Fix

I CAN'T WORK MY WAY INTO HEAVEN. I MUST BE FORGIVEN.

LUKE 12:32(NASB)

"Do not be afraid, little flock, for your Father has chosen gladly to give you the kingdom."

MATTHEW 11:25(NIV)

"At that time Jesus said, 'I praise you, Father, Lord of heaven and earth, because you have hidden these things from the wise and learned, and revealed them to little children. Yes, Father, for this was your good pleasure.'"

....

....

....

....

....

....

....

....

....

....

....

....

....

JUNKIE FIX

....

GOD GLADLY GIVES ENTRY TO HEAVEN TO HIS SAINTS.

LUKE 5:20(NIV)

"When Jesus saw their faith, he said, "Friend, your sins are forgiven."

Junkie Fix

Faith is critical.

LUKE 21:15(NIV)

"For I will give you words and wisdom that none of your adversaries will be able to resist or contradict."

ACTS 6:10(NIV)

"None of them was able to stand against the wisdom and Spirit by which Stephen spoke."

JUNKIE FIX

THE WORDS GOD GIVES ME ARE PERFECT, BETTER THAN ANYTHING I COULD PREPARE.

LUKE 6:46(NASB)

"Why do you call Me, 'Lord, Lord,' and do not do what I say?

MATTHEW 7:21(NIV)

"Not everyone who says to me, 'Lord, Lord,' will enter the kingdom of heaven, but only he who does the will of my Father who is in heaven."

JUNKIE FIX

JESUS ASKS ME TO DO MORE THAN SAY "HE IS THE LORD!"

MARK 11:24(NKJV)

"Therefore I say to you, whatever things you ask when you pray, believe that you receive them, and you will have them."

MATTHEW 7:7(NIV)

"Ask and it will be given to you; seek and you will find; knock and the door will be opened to you."

JOHN 14:13(NKJV)

"And whatever you ask in My name, that I will do, that the Father may be glorified in the Son."

JOHN 15:7(NKJV)

"If you abide in Me, and My words abide in you, you will ask what you desire, and it shall be done for you."

JOHN 16:24(NKJV)

"Until now you have asked nothing in My name. Ask, and you will receive, that your joy may be full."

JAMES 1:6(NASB)

"But he must ask in faith without any doubting, for the one who doubts is like the surf of the sea, driven and tossed by the wind."

....

....

....

....

Junkie Fix

"Ask and believe!" Simple, isn't it?

LUKE 6:21(NKJV)

"Blessed are you who hunger now, For you shall be filled. Blessed are you who weep now, For you shall laugh."

PSALM 126:5(NLT)

"Those who plant in tears will harvest with shouts of joy."

ISAIAH 61:3(NKJV)

"To console those who mourn in Zion, To give them beauty for ashes, The oil of joy for mourning, The garment of praise for the spirit of heaviness; That they may be called trees of righteousness, The planting of the Lord, that He may be glorified."

ISAIAH 65:13(NIV)

"Therefore this is what the Sovereign Lord says 'My servants will eat, but you will go hungry; my servants will drink, but you will go thirsty; my servants will rejoice, but you will be put to shame.'"

MATTHEW 5:6(WEB)

"Blessed are they who hunger and thirst for righteousness for they shall be filled."

REVELATION 7:16(NIV)

"Never again will they hunger; never again will they thirst. The sun will not beat upon them, nor any scorching heat. For the Lamb at the center of the throne will be their shepherd; he will lead them to springs of living water. And God will wipe away every tear from their eyes."

Junkie Fix

My belief in the Lord comforts me that all trials are temporary. Rejoicing is coming.

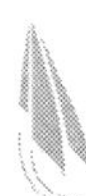

LUKE 1:79(NIV)

"To shine on those living in darkness and in the shadow of death, to guide our feet into the path of peace."

ISAIAH 9:2(NKJV)

"The people who walked in darkness Have seen a great light; Those who dwelt in the land of the shadow of death, Upon them a light has shined."

ACTS 26:18(NKJV)

"to open their eyes, in order to turn them from darkness to light, and from the power of Satan to God, that they may receive forgiveness of sins and an inheritance among those who are sanctified by faith in Me."

2CORINTHIANS 4:6(NASB)

"For God, who said, "Light shall shine out of darkness," is the One who has shone in our hearts to give the Light of the knowledge of the glory of God in the face of Christ."

EPHESIANS 5:14(NIV)

"For it is light that makes everything visible. This is why it is said 'Wake up, O sleeper, rise from the dead, and Christ will shine on you.'"

JOHN 14:27(NLT)

"I am leaving you with a gift--peace of mind and heart. And the peace I give isn't like the peace the world gives. So, don't be troubled or afraid."

JUNKIE FIX

GOD SHINES A LIGHT ON THE DARK PLACES OF MY SOUL, REVEALING WHAT IS WRONG. I CAN TURN, FOLLOWING HIM, LEAVING THAT DARKNESS... FINDING PEACE IN HIM.

LUKE 1:47(NASB)

"And my spirit has rejoiced in God my Savior."

PSALM 35:9(NKJV)

"And my soul shall be joyful in the Lord; It shall rejoice in His salvation."

HABAKKUK 3:18(NLT)

"Yet I will rejoice in the Lord! I will be joyful in the God of my salvation."

1TIMOTHY 2:4(NLT)

"For he wants everyone to be saved and to understand the truth.

TITUS 1:2(WEB)

"In hope of eternal life, which God, who cannot lie, promised before the world began;"

TITUS 2:10(NIV)

"And not to steal from them, but to show that they can be fully trusted, so that in every way they will make the teaching about God our Savior attractive."

JUDE 1:25(NIV)

"To the only God our Savior be glory, majesty, power, and authority, through Jesus Christ our Lord, before all ages, now and for evermore! Amen."

Junkie Fix

Where and why else would I rejoice? God is that great.

LUKE 1:53(NKJV)

"He has filled the hungry with good things, And the rich He has sent away empty."

MATTHEW 5:6(NIV)

"Blessed are those who hunger and thirst for righteousness, for they will be filled."

MARK 10:24(NKJV)

"And the disciples were astonished at His words. But Jesus answered again and said to them, 'Children, how hard it is for those who trust in riches to enter the kingdom of God! It is easier for a camel to go through the eye of a needle than for a rich man to enter the kingdom of God.'"

....

....

....

....

....

....

....

....

JUNKIE FIX

....

IF I SEEK HIM, I WILL BE FILLED WITH HIM. IF I AM FILLED WITH ANYTHING ELSE, I WILL STAY EMPTY ... AND DEAD.

LUKE 5:31(NIV)

"Jesus answered them, 'It is not the healthy who need a doctor, but the sick.'"

HOSEA 6:6(NKJV)

"For I desire mercy and not sacrifice, And the knowledge of God more than burnt offerings."

JUNKIE FIX

JESUS DIDN'T COME TO PLAY RELIGION. HE CAME TO SAVE THE LOST!

Mark 14:34(NIV)

"'My soul is overwhelmed with sorrow to the point of death,' he said to them. 'Stay here and keep watch.'"

Isaiah 53:3(NKJV)

"He is despised and rejected by men, A Man of sorrows and acquainted with grief. And we hid, as it were, our faces from Him; He was despised, and we did not esteem Him. Surely, He has borne our grief and carried our sorrows; yet, we esteemed Him stricken, Smitten by God, and afflicted."

....

....

....

....

....

....

....

....

....

....

....

....

Junkie Fix

....

Even Jesus struggled.

MARK 9:24(NKJV)

"Immediately the father of the child cried out and said with tears, 'Lord, I believe; help my unbelief!'"

LUKE 17:5(NASB)

"The apostles said to the Lord, 'Increase our faith!'"

JUNKIE FIX

I ASK THE LORD FOR THE FAITH HE WANTS ME TO HAVE.

LUKE 6:22(NIV)

"Blessed are you when men hate you, when they exclude you and insult you and reject your name as evil, because of the Son of Man."

MATTHEW 5:11(NASB)

"Blessed are you when people insult you and persecute you, and falsely say all kinds of evil against you because of Me."

1 PETER 2:19(NLT)

"For God is pleased with you when, for the sake of your conscience, you patiently endure unfair treatment."

1 PETER 3:14(NIV)

"But even if you should suffer for what is right, you are blessed. Do not fear what they fear; do not be frightened."

1 PETER 4:14(NKJV)

"If you are reproached for the name of Christ, blessed are you, for the Spirit of glory and of God rests upon you. On their part, He is blasphemed, but on your part, He is glorified."

Junkie Fix

Being attacked simply because I am a Christian... is an experience that blesses.

PROVERBS 8:36(NKJV)

"But he who sins against me wrongs his own soul; All those who hate me love death."

JUNKIE FIX

SINNING AGAINST GOD(OR MAN) MEANS I WANT TO GO TO HELL.

ECCLESIASTES 1:3(NKJV)

"What profit has a man from all his labor in which he toils under the sun?"

JUNKIE FIX

WHEN I THINK BEYOND THIS LIFE, ONLY GOD CAN BRING PROFIT THAT LASTS.

ACTS 5:38(NKJV)

"And now I say to you, keep away from these men and let them alone; for if this plan or this work is of men, it will come to nothing; but if it is of God, you cannot overthrow it--lest you even be found to fight against God."

1 CORINTHIANS 1:25(NIV)

"For the foolishness of God is wiser than man's wisdom, and the weakness of God is stronger than man's strength."

JUNKIE FIX

DON'T FIGHT GOD! EVEN ON A BAD DAY, HE WINS.

MARK 5:36(NKJV)

"As soon as Jesus heard the word that was spoken, He said to the ruler of the synagogue, 'Do not be afraid; only believe.'"

JUNKIE FIX

JUST BELIEVE. THERE IS NOTHING TO WORRY ABOUT.

MARK 2:17(NKJV)

"When Jesus heard it, He said to them, 'Those who are well have no need of a physician, but those who are sick. I did not come to call the righteous, but sinners, to repentance.'"

MATTHEW 18:11(NKJV)

"For the Son of Man has come to save that which was lost."

JUNKIE FIX

JESUS CAME TO SAVE ME FROM THE SIN I HAVE. HE HELPS ME TURN FROM IT.

Acts 4:12(NLT)

"There is salvation in no one else! There is no other name in all of heaven for people to call on to save them."

Matthew 1:21(NKJV)

"And she will bring forth a Son, and you shall call His name JESUS, for He will save His people from their sins.

1Timothy 2:5(NKJV)

"For there is one God and one Mediator between God and men, the Man Christ Jesus."

Junkie Fix

Doing good or being great ... just isn't enough.

MARK 2:27(NKJV)

"And He said to them, 'The Sabbath was made for man, and not man for the Sabbath. Therefore the Son of Man is also Lord of the Sabbath.'"

JUNKIE FIX

THE DAY OF REST WAS MADE TO BE A BLESSING.

ACTS 8:20(NKJV)

"But Peter said to him, 'Your money perish with you, because you thought that the gift of God could be purchased with money! You have neither part nor portion in this matter, for your heart is not right in the sight of God. Repent therefore of this your wickedness, and pray God if perhaps the thought of your heart may be forgiven you. For I see that you are poisoned by bitterness and bound by iniquity.'"

JUNKIE FIX

I CAN'T BUY GOD.

LUKE 12:20(NIV)

"But God said to him, 'You fool! This very night your life will be demanded from you. Then who will get what you have prepared for yourself?'"

JOB 27:8(NKJV)

"For what is the hope of the hypocrite, Though he may gain much, If God takes away his life?"

PSALM 39:6(NLT)

"We are merely moving shadows, and all our busy rushing ends in nothing. We heap up wealth for someone else to spend."

PSALM 52:7(NKJV)

"Here is the man who did not make God his strength, But trusted in the abundance of his riches, And strengthened himself in his wickedness."

JEREMIAH 17:11(NASB)

"As a partridge that hatches eggs which it has not laid, So is he who makes a fortune, but unjustly; In the midst of his days it will forsake him, And in the end he will be a fool."

1TIMOTHY 6:18(NASB)

"Instruct them to do good, to be rich in good works, to be generous and ready to share, storing up for themselves the treasure of a good foundation for the future, so that they may take hold of that which is life indeed."

JAMES 2:5(NIV)

"Listen, my dear brothers Has not God chosen those who are poor in the eyes of the world to be rich in faith and to inherit the kingdom he promised those who love him?"

JAMES 5:1(NASB)

"Come now, you rich, weep and howl for your miseries which are coming upon you. Your riches have rotted and your garments have become moth-eaten. Your gold and your silver have rusted; and their rust will be a witness against you and will consume your flesh like fire. It is in the last days that you have stored up your treasure! Behold, the pay of the laborers who mowed your fields, and which has been withheld by you, cries out against you; and the outcry of those who did the harvesting has reached the ears of the Lord of Sabbath. You have lived luxuriously on the earth and led a life of wanton pleasure; you have fattened your hearts in a day of slaughter."

....

....

....

....

....

JUNKIE FIX

....

MY LIFE IS SHORT. I VALUE WHAT GOD GAVE ME BY INVESTING IN THE ETERNAL.

God is so powerful He can do anything. What's my part? I must have faith and believe. I need to do more than speak words. I have to live the words God has spoken to me.

I have grown to realize how short life is. My troubles won't last forever. I can be wrapped up in them, a wondering soul helping no one, consumed with self-pity or I can believe Jesus is my peace. I know God is fair and I don't deserve grace, but Jesus gives it, if I have the faith to accept it. I know that if I don't have enough faith I can ask for more.

I must be forgiven because I am doomed without grace. Playing Christian just doesn't cut it He knows our hearts better than we know ourselves. Being saved means being bound to Jesus Christ, turning over control. It is okay that I struggle, even Jesus struggled, but once I believe, there is nothing else to worry about. Just believe.

Fleshy Fixes

Earthly desires and things about me as a person

ROMANS 5:19(NKJV)

"For as by one man's disobedience many were made sinners, so also by one Man's obedience many will be made righteous."

Junkie Fix

Everyone fails at living perfectly but it took Christ to make everything right again.

ACTS 17:27(NKJV)

"So that they should seek the Lord, in the hope that they might grope for Him and find Him, though He is not far from each one of us;"

ROMANS 1:20(NIV)

"For since the creation of the world God's invisible qualities—his eternal power and divine nature—have been clearly seen, being understood from what has been made, so that men are without excuse."

ACTS 14:17(NIV)

"Yet he has not left himself without testimony He has shown kindness by giving you rain from heaven and crops in their seasons; he provides you with plenty of food and fills your hearts with joy."

JUNKIE FIX

GOD SHOWS HIMSELF ALL AROUND ME, BUT IF I SEE HIM I HAVE TO BELIEVE IN HIM. THAT IS WHY SOME REFUSE TO RECOGNIZE HIM AND HIS WORK.

ROMANS 5:10(NIV)

"For if, when we were God's enemies, we were reconciled to him through the death of his Son, how much more, having been reconciled, shall we be saved through his life! Not only is this so, but we also rejoice in God through our Lord Jesus Christ, through whom we have now received reconciliation."

Junkie Fix

I sinned and God loved, then I loved and God held me close.

ROMANS 2:21(NIV)

"You, then, who teach others, do you not teach yourself? You who preach against stealing, do you steal?"

PROVERBS 11:9(NKJV)

"The hypocrite with his mouth destroys his neighbor, but through knowledge, the righteous will be delivered."

JAMES 3:1(NASB)

"Let not many of you become teachers, my brethren, knowing that as such we will incur a stricter judgment."

JUNKIE FIX

NON-CHRISTIANS CURSE GOD'S NAME BECAUSE OF BAD TEACHERS.

ROMANS 5:8(NLT)

"But God showed his great love for us by sending Christ to die for us while we were still sinners."

John 15:13(NASB)

"Greater love has no one than this, that one lay down his life for his friends.

....

....

....

....

....

....

....

....

....

....

....

....

....

....

....

Junkie Fix

....

God loves us, when we fall, when we hate, and while we live.

ROMANS 2:7(NIV)

"To those who by persistence in doing good seek glory, honor, and immortality, he will give eternal life. But for those who are self-seeking and who reject the truth and follow evil, there will be wrath and anger."

JUNKIE FIX

EVERYDAY I CHOOSE WHICH SIDE I WILL BE ON.

ROMANS 1:31(NLT)

"They refuse to understand, break their promises, and are heartless and unforgiving. They are fully aware of God's death penalty for those who do these things, yet they go right ahead and do them anyway. And, worse yet, they encourage others to do them, too."

JUNKIE FIX

EVIL IS EVIL AND SO IS LOOKING THE OTHER WAY.

ACTS 24:25(NASB)

"But as he was discussing righteousness, self-control and the judgment to come, Felix became frightened and said, 'Go away for the present, and when I find time I will summon you.'"

JUNKIE FIX

FEELING FEAR WHEN FACING OUR FAULTS MAKES US PUSH AWAY GOD AND HIS PEOPLE BUT GOD DOESN'T HAVE TO WAIT.

ACTS 26:15(NKJV)

"So I said, 'Who are You, Lord?' And He said, 'I am Jesus, whom you are persecuting. But rise and stand on your feet; for I have appeared to you for this purpose, to make you a minister and a witness both of the things, which you have seen, and of the things that I will yet reveal to you.'"

PHILIPPIANS 3:6(NKJV)

"Concerning zeal, persecuting the church; concerning the righteousness, which is in the law, blameless. But what things were gain to me, these I have counted loss for Christ. Yet indeed I also count all things loss for the excellence of the knowledge of Christ Jesus my Lord, for whom I have suffered the loss of all things, and count them as rubbish, that I may gain Christ"

....

....

....

....

....

....

....

....

JUNKIE FIX

....

IT'S NOT WHO I WAS THAT IS IMPORTANT BUT WHO HE MAKES ME TO BE.

LUKE 16:13(NIV)

"No servant can serve two masters. Either he will hate the one and love the other, or he will be devoted to the one and despise the other. You cannot serve both God and Money."

GALATIANS 1:10(NIV)

"Am I now trying to win the approval of men, or of God? Or am I trying to please men? If I were still trying to please men, I would not be a servant of Christ."

....

....

....

....

....

....

....

....

....

....

....

....

....

JUNKIE FIX

....

I WILL SERVE THE LORD! HE WILL NOT HONOR ME IF HE IS SECOND TO ANYTHING IN MY LIFE.

ACTS 19:19(NASB)

"And many of those who practiced magic brought their books together and began burning them in the sight of everyone; and they counted up the price of them and found it fifty thousand pieces of silver. So, the word of the Lord was growing mightily and prevailing."

Junkie Fix

God didn't force them to burn their expensive magic books. Neither did Christians. They burned their own books.

LUKE 22:53(NKJV)

"When I was with you daily in the temple, you did not try to seize Me. But this is your hour, and the power of darkness."

LUKE 20:19(NKJV)

"And the chief priests and the scribes that very hour sought to lay hands on Him, but they feared the people—for they knew He had spoken this parable against them."

JOHN 8:37(NKJV)

"I know that you are Abraham's descendants, but you seek to kill Me, because My word has no place in you."

JUNKIE FIX

THIS WAS THE TIME FOR THEM TO CHOOSE, AND THEY CHOOSE TO BE PAWNS OF DARKNESS.

Luke 18:7(WEB)

"And shall not God avenge his own elect, which cry day and night unto him, though he bear long with them?"

Revelations 6:10(NIV)

"They called out in a loud voice, "How long, Sovereign Lord, holy and true, until you judge the inhabitants of the earth and avenge our blood?"

....

....

....

....

....

....

....

....

....

....

....

....

....

....

....

Junkie Fix

....

God shall avenge the martyrs in His time.

LUKE 22:48(NKJV)

"But Jesus said to him, "Judas, are you betraying the Son of Man with a kiss?"

MARK 14:21(NASB)

"For the Son of Man is to go just as it is written of Him; but woe to that man by whom the Son of Man is betrayed! It would have been good for that man if he had not been born."

JUNKIE FIX

JESUS KNEW THE FUTURE. HE REMINDED JUDAS OF THE CONSEQUENCES OF HIS CHOICE.

LUKE 13:24(NASB)

"Strive to enter through the narrow door; for many, I tell you, will seek to enter and will not be able."

JOHN 7:34(NKJV)

"You will seek Me and not find Me, and where I am you cannot come."

JOHN 8:21(NLT)

"Later Jesus said to them again, 'I am going away. You will search for me and die in your sin. You cannot come where I am going.'"

JUNKIE FIX

I WILL SEEK JESUS WHILE THERE IS STILL TIME, I CANNOT REACH HEAVEN ON MY OWN.

LUKE 6:36(NIV)

"Be merciful, just as your Father is merciful."

MATTHEW 5:48(NKJV)

"Therefore you shall be perfect, just as your Father in heaven is perfect."

EPHESIANS 4:32(NKJV)

"And be kind to one another, tenderhearted, forgiving one another, even as God in Christ forgave you."

....

....

....

....

....

....

....

....

....

....

....

....

....

JUNKIE FIX

....

IN LIFE, GOD IS OUR EXAMPLE.

LUKE 18:39(NLT)

"The crowds ahead of Jesus tried to hush the man, but he only shouted louder, 'Son of David, have mercy on me!'"

MATTHEW 10:28(NASB)

"Do not fear those who kill the body but are unable to kill the soul; but rather fear Him who is able to destroy both soul and body in hell."

JUNKIE FIX

WHEN ANYONE TELLS ME TO STOP PROCLAIMING CHRIST, DO I STOP OR DO I CRY OUT MORE?

LUKE 3:11(NIV)

"John answered, 'The man with two tunics should share with him who has none, and the one who has food should do the same.'"

2 CORINTHIANS 8:14(NASB)

"At this present time your abundance being a supply for their need, so that their abundance also may become a supply for your need, that there may be equality."

1 JOHN 3:17(NASB)

"But whoever has the world's goods, and sees his brother in need and closes his heart against him, how does the love of God abide in him?"

1 JOHN 4:20(NASB)

If someone says, "I love God," and hates his brother, he is a liar; for the one who does not love his brother whom he has seen, cannot love God whom he has not seen.

1 TIMOTHY 6:17(NIV)

"Command those who are rich in this present world not to be arrogant nor to put their hope in wealth, which is so uncertain, but to put their hope in God, who richly provides us with everything for our enjoyment. Command them to do good, to be rich in good deeds, and to be generous and willing to share."

....

....

....

Junkie Fix

I need to rise to the earthly needs of others.

LUKE 12:23(NIV)

"Life is more than food, and the body more than clothes."

MATTHEW 6:30(NASB)

"But if God so clothes the grass of the field, which is alive today and tomorrow is thrown into the furnace, will He not much more clothe you? You of little faith!"

MATTHEW 8:26(NKJV)

"But He said to them, 'Why are you fearful, O you of little faith?' Then He arose and rebuked the winds and the sea, and there was a great calm."

MATTHEW 14:31(NIV)

"Immediately Jesus reached out his hand and caught him. 'You of little faith,' he said, 'why did you doubt?'"

MATTHEW 16:8(NLT)

"Jesus knew what they were thinking, so he said, 'You have so little faith! Why are you worried about having no food?'"

....

....

....

....

JUNKIE FIX

....

LIFE IS MORE THAN PHYSICAL. GOD PROVIDES FOR ALL NEEDS.

Luke 23:34(NASB)

"But Jesus was saying, 'Father, forgive them; for they do not know what they are doing.' And they cast lots, dividing up His garments among themselves."

Psalm 109:4(NLT)

"I love them, but they try to destroy me––even as I am praying for them!"

Matthew 5:44(NKJV)

"But I say to you, love your enemies, bless those who curse you, do good to those who hate you, and pray for those who spitefully use you and persecute you."

1Corinthians 4:12(NIV)

"We work hard with our own hands. When we are cursed, we bless; when we are persecuted, we endure it."

....

....

....

....

....

....

Junkie Fix

I PRAY WITH BROKENHEARTED GRIEVING FOR MY PERSECUTORS, THEY CAN'T UNDERSTAND WHAT WILL HAPPEN BECAUSE OF THEIR HATE.

LUKE 3:9(NASB)

"Indeed the axe is already laid at the root of the trees; so every tree that does not bear good fruit is cut down and thrown into the fire."

GALATIANS 5:19(NIV)

"The acts of the sinful nature are obvious sexual immorality, impurity and debauchery; idolatry and witchcraft; hatred, discord, jealousy, fits of rage, selfish ambition, dissensions, factions and envy; drunkenness, orgies, and the like. I warn you, as I did before, that those who live like this will not inherit the kingdom of God."

JUNKIE FIX

WHAT FRUIT AM I BEARING? I MUST MAKE MY ACTIONS LEADING ME TO MY GOAL. MY FLESH WILL LEAD ME INTO THE FIRE.

LUKE 5:5(NASB)

"Simon answered and said, 'Master, we worked hard all night and caught nothing, but I will do as You say and let down the nets.'"

Junkie Fix

I must put God's requests before my desires. He will bless my faithfulness.

LUKE 13:3(NIV)

"I tell you, no! But unless you repent, you too will all perish."

2CORINTHIANS 6:2(NKJV)

"For He says 'In an acceptable time I have heard you, and in the day of salvation I have helped you.' Behold, now is the accepted time; behold, now is the day of salvation."

JUNKIE FIX

ALL SIN BRINGS DEATH AND THE TIME TO TURN FROM IT IS NOW.

LUKE 12:2(NASB)

"But there is nothing covered up that will not be revealed, and hidden that will not be known."

MARK 4:22(NKJV)

"For there is nothing hidden which will not be revealed, nor has anything been kept secret but that it should come to light."

LUKE 12:3(NLT)

"Whatever you have said in the dark will be heard in the light and what you have whispered behind closed doors will be shouted from the housetops for all to hear!"

1 CORINTHIANS 4:5(NASB)

"Therefore do not go on passing judgment before the time, but wait until the Lord comes who will both bring to light the things hidden in the darkness and disclose the motives of men's hearts; and then each man's praise will come to him from God."

....

....

....

....

JUNKIE FIX

....

GOD KNOWS ALL AND ONE DAY EVERYONE WILL KNOW WHAT I TRIED TO HIDE.

MARK 15:15(NKJV)

"So Pilate, wanting to gratify the crowd, released Barabbas to them; and he delivered Jesus, after he had scourged Him, to be crucified."

ISAIAH 50:6(NKJV)

"I gave My back to those who struck Me, And My cheeks to those who plucked out the beard; I did not hide My face from shame and spitting."

ISAIAH 53:8(NKJV)

"He was taken from prison and from judgment, and who will declare His generation? For He was cut off from the land of the living; for the transgressions of My people He was stricken."

JUNKIE FIX

WHO DO I FEAR? WHO DO I GRATIFY?

MARK 9:49(NKJV)

"For everyone will be seasoned with fire, and every sacrifice will be seasoned with salt."

Junkie Fix

Everyone in life suffers but Christians will be purified and every sacrifice will be preserved for God.

ECCLESIASTES 7:16(NKJV)

"Do not be overly righteous, Nor be overly wise Why should you destroy yourself?"

ROMANS 12:3(NIV)

"For by the grace given me I say to every one of you Do not think of yourself more highly than you ought, but rather think of yourself with sober judgment, in accordance with the measure of faith God has given you."

JUNKIE FIX

THIS IS MY WARNING AGAINST THE SELF-RIGHTEOUS AND POMPOUS. I CANNOT GET MYSELF TO HEAVEN NO MATTER HOW GOOD I AM.

LUKE 6:24(NIV)

"But woe to you who are rich, for you have already received your comfort."

MATTHEW 6:2(NASB)

"So when you give to the poor, do not sound a trumpet before you, as the hypocrites do in the synagogues and in the streets, so that they may be honored by men. Truly, I say to you, they have their reward in full."

LUKE 12:21(NKJV)

"So is he who lays up treasure for himself, and is not rich toward God."

JAMES 5:2(NASB)

"Your riches have rotted and your garments have become moth-eaten. Your gold and your silver have rusted; and their rust will be a witness against you and will consume your flesh like fire. It is in the last days that you have stored up your treasure! Behold, the pay of the laborers who mowed your fields, and which has been withheld by you, cries out against you; and the outcry of those who did the harvesting has reached the ears of the Lord of Sabbath. You have lived luxuriously on the earth and led a life of wanton pleasure; you have fattened your hearts in a day of slaughter."

JUNKIE FIX

WHEN RICHES REACH MY HEART, I CANNOT ESCAPE DEATH.

Ecclesiastes 4:10(NIV)

"If one falls down, his friend can help him up. But pity the man who falls and has no one to help him up!"

Junkie Fix

Life is richer with a godly friend.

PROVERBS 20:12(NLT)

"Ears to hear and eyes to see--both are gifts from the Lord."

EXODUS 4:11(NASB)

"The Lord said to him, 'Who has made man's mouth? Or who makes him mute or deaf, or seeing or blind? Is it not I, the Lord?'"

JUNKIE FIX

GOD SEES AND HEARS EVERYTHING. HE MADE MY SENSES.

PROVERBS 27:20(NKJV)

"Hell and Destruction are never full; so the eyes of man are never satisfied."

PROVERBS 30:15(NIV)

"The leech has two daughters. 'Give! Give!' they cry. There are three things that are never satisfied, four that never say, 'Enough!' the grave, the barren womb, land, which is never satisfied with water, and fire, which never says, 'Enough!'"

ECCLESIASTES 4:8(NKJV)

"There is one alone, without companion He has neither son nor brother. Yet, there is no end to all his labors, nor is his eye satisfied with riches. But he never asks, 'For whom do I toil and deprive myself of good?' This also is vanity and a grave misfortune."

HABAKKUK 2:5(NASB)

"Furthermore, wine betrays the haughty man, So that he does not stay at home. He enlarges his appetite like Sheol, and he is like death, never satisfied. He also gathers to himself all nations and collects to himself all peoples."

....

....

....

....

....

Junkie Fix

I can never sin enough to be satisfied, just like the place of punishment, Hell will never over flow.

LUKE 11:26(NASB)

"Then it goes and takes along seven other spirits more evil than itself, and they go in and live there; and the last state of that man becomes worse than the first."

JOHN 5:14(NKJV)

"Afterward Jesus found him in the temple, and said to him, 'See, you have been made well. Sin no more, lest a worse thing come upon you.'"

HEBREWS 6:4(NKJV)

"For it is impossible for those who were once enlightened, and have tasted the heavenly gift, and have become partakers of the Holy Spirit, and have tasted the good word of God and the powers of the age to come, if they fall away, to renew them again to repentance, since they crucify again for themselves the Son of God, and put Him to an open shame."

HEBREWS 10:26(NASB)

"For if we go on sinning willfully after receiving the knowledge of the truth, there no longer remains a sacrifice for sins, but a terrifying expectation of judgment and the fury of a fire which will consume the adversaries. Anyone who has set aside the Law of Moses dies without mercy on the testimony of two or three witnesses. How much severer punishment do you think he will deserve who has trampled under foot the Son of God, and has regarded as unclean the blood of the covenant by which he was sanctified, and has insulted the Spirit of grace?"

2 Peter 2:20 (NKJV)

"For if, after they have escaped the pollutions of the world through the knowledge of the Lord and Savior Jesus Christ, they are again entangled in them and overcome, the latter end is worse for them than the beginning."

Junkie Fix

IF I RETURN TO EVIL AFTER GOD HAS MADE ME CLEAN, IT IS MUCH WORSE FOR ME.

Mark 7:23 (NLT)

"All these vile things come from within; they are what defile you and make you unacceptable to God."

Proverbs 4:23 (NKJV)

Keep your heart with all diligence, for out of it spring the issues of life.

Junkie Fix

Evil comes from inside and must be cleaned out before it spills out.

ACTS 1:25(NKJV)

"To take part in this ministry and apostleship from which Judas by transgression fell, that he might go to his own place."

ACTS 1:18(NIV)

"With the reward he got for his wickedness, Judas bought a field; there he fell headlong, his body burst open and all his intestines spilled out. Everyone in Jerusalem heard about this, so they called that field in their language Akeldama, that is, Field of Blood."

MATTHEW 26:24(NIV)

"The Son of Man will go just as it is written about him. But woe to that man who betrays the Son of Man! It would be better for him if he had not been born."

....

....

....

....

....

....

....

....

JUNKIE FIX

....

BETTER TO BE FORGOTTEN THEN REMEMBERED LIKE THAT.

Acts 5:3(NASB)

"But Peter said, 'Ananias, why has Satan filled your heart to lie to the Holy Spirit and to keep back some of the price of the land? "While it remained unsold, did it not remain your own? And after it was sold, was it not under your control? Why is it that you have conceived this deed in your heart? You have not lied to men but to God.' And as he heard these words, Ananias fell down and breathed his last; and great fear came over all who heard of it."

Deuteronomy 23:21(NLT)

"When you make a vow to the Lord your God, be prompt in doing whatever you promised him. For the Lord your God demands that you promptly fulfill all your vows. If you don't, you will be guilty of sin.

....

....

....

....

....

....

....

....

Junkie Fix

....

When it comes to promises God doesn't mess around.

ACTS 2:3(NLT)

"Then, what looked like flames or tongues of fire appeared and settled on each of them."

EXODUS 3:2(NIV)

"There the angel of the Lord appeared to him in flames of fire from within a bush. Moses saw that though the bush was on fire it did not burn up."

JUNKIE FIX

MAN, GOD HAS STYLE.

Acts 3:19(NASB)

"Therefore repent and return, so that your sins may be wiped away, in order that times of refreshing may come from the presence of the Lord; and that He may send Jesus, the Christ appointed for you."

1 Peter 2:24(NIV)

"He himself bore our sins in his body on the tree, so that we might die to sins and live for righteousness; by his wounds you have been healed."

Isaiah 43:25(NASB)

"I, even I, am the one who wipes out your transgressions for My own sake, And I will not remember your sins."

Isaiah 44:22(NKJV)

I have blotted out, like a thick cloud, your transgressions, and like a cloud, your sins. Return to Me, for I have redeemed you."

....

....

....

....

....

Junkie Fix

....

I accept that being forgiven was hard but Jesus said, "It is finished."

At the root of Fleshy Fixes is "I choose." Every moment I choose good or evil. That is free will. God doesn't force us to do what is right. Being faithful would be a lot easier if He did, but force is not Love. God knows I am not perfect. He made me. I remember God is the judge.

When it comes to how I feel about others I have to remember a few things. Those who hate me don't know they are damning themselves, just as if I am turning my back on God when I turn my back on them. God did not call me to hate my neighbors but to love them so I volunteer to humble myself and share the only way to avoid getting what we deserve. I choose to share Jesus as Lord and Savior, just as a kind soul did for me.

I did not write this section to wallow in hate and damnation but to remind myself how good things are when I am faithful and why I need to stay on track with God. It is so easy to get lost.

Mental Fixes

Wisdom and Understanding

ROMANS 4:4(NKJV)

"Now to him who works, the wages are not counted as grace but as debt."

EPHESIANS 2:8(NASB)

"For by grace you have been saved through faith; and that not of yourselves, it is the gift of God; not as a result of works, so that no one may boast."

JUNKIE FIX

I CAN'T MAKE OR BUY GRACE. IT IS GIVEN TO ME FROM GOD.

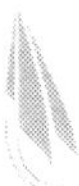

ROMANS 6:17(NKJV)

"But God be thanked that though you were slaves of sin, yet you obeyed from the heart that form of doctrine to which you were delivered."

2TIMOTHY 1:13(NASB)

"Retain the standard of sound words, which you have heard from me, in the faith and love which are in Christ Jesus."

PSALM 119:11(NIV)

"I have hidden your word in my heart that I might not sin against you."

JUNKIE FIX

GOD'S WORD IS MORE THAN A BOOK; IT'S WORDS FROM GOD FOR ME.

ROMANS 1:23(NASB)

"And exchanged the glory of the incorruptible God for an image in the form of corruptible man and of birds and four-footed animals and crawling creatures."

Jeremiah 2:11(NLT)

"Has any nation ever exchanged its gods for another god, even though its gods are nothing? Yet, my people have exchanged their glorious God for worthless idols!"

Junkie Fix

God is perfect. That thought is so beyond my understanding but I can't pretend He is anything else.

ROMANS 1:14(NASB)

"I am under obligation both to Greeks and to barbarians, both to the wise and to the foolish. So, for my part, I am eager to preach the gospel to you also who are in Rome."

Acts 9:15(NASB)

"But the Lord said to him, "Go, for he is a chosen instrument of Mine, to bear My name before the Gentiles and kings and the sons of Israel;"

....

....

....

....

....

....

....

....

....

....

....

....

....

Junkie Fix

....

The knowledge and understanding I have of Christ I have to pass on to others.

ROMANS 1:7(NIV)

"To all in Rome who are loved by God and called to be saints Grace and peace to you from God our Father and from the Lord Jesus Christ."

2TIMOTHY 1:9(NIV)

"Who has saved us and called us to a holy life—not because of anything we have done but because of his own purpose and grace. This grace was given us in Christ Jesus before the beginning of time."

....

....

....

....

....

....

....

....

....

....

....

....

....

JUNKIE FIX

GOD IS INFINITE AND FULL OF GRACE. HE KNEW THAT WE WOULD BE TOGETHER BEFORE HE STARTED TIME.

ROMANS 1:10(WEB)

"Making request(if by any means now at length I may have a prosperous journey by the will of God) to come to you."

MATTHEW 6:10(NKJV)

"Your kingdom come. Your will be done on earth as it is in heaven."

JAMES 4:14(NKJV)

"Whereas you do not know what will happen tomorrow. For what is your life? It is even a vapor that appears for a little time and then vanishes away. Instead, you ought to say, 'If the Lord wills, we shall live and do this or that.'"

....

....

....

....

....

....

....

....

JUNKIE FIX

I DON'T PRETEND I AM IN CHARGE.

Acts 27:25(NIV)

"So keep up your courage, men, for I have faith in God that it will happen just as he told me."

Luke 1:45(NKJV)

"Blessed is she who believed, for there will be a fulfillment of those things which were told her from the Lord."

Junkie Fix

If I can't trust God, who can I trust?

ACTS 24:15(NIV)

"And I have the same hope in God as these men, that there will be a resurrection of both the righteous and the wicked. So, I strive always to keep my conscience clear before God and man."

JOHN 5:28(NIV)

"Do not be amazed at this, for a time is coming when all who are in their graves will hear his voice and come out—those who have done good will rise to live, and those who have done evil will rise to be condemned."

JUNKIE FIX

THIS BEING SO... NO QUESTION AND NO DOUBT.

Acts 20:34(NLT)

"You know that these hands of mine have worked to pay my own way, and I have even supplied the needs of those who were with me. And I have been a constant example of how you can help the poor by working hard. You should remember the words of the Lord Jesus
'It is more blessed to give than to receive.'"

Ephesians 4:28(NASB)

"He who steals must steal no longer; but rather he must labor, performing with his own hands what is good, so that he will have something to share with one who has need."

1Thessalonians 2:9(NKJV)

"For you remember, brethren, our labor and toil; for laboring night and day, that we might not be a burden to any of you, we preached to you the gospel of God."

....

....

....

....

....

....

Junkie Fix

....

Great reasons to go to work on days when I don't want to get out of bed.

ACTS 19:11(NKJV)

"Now God worked unusual miracles by the hands of Paul, so that even handkerchiefs or aprons were brought from his body to the sick, and the diseases left them and the evil spirits went out of them. Then some of the itinerant Jewish exorcists took it upon themselves to call the name of the Lord Jesus over those who had evil spirits, saying, 'We exorcise you by the Jesus whom Paul preaches.'"

Junkie Fix

God can do what He wants and sometimes it does surprise me.

ACTS 17:26(NKJV)

"And He has made from one blood every nation of men to dwell on all the face of the earth, and has determined their preappointed times and the boundaries of their dwellings."

Junkie Fix

God makes people and countries. He knows when they begin, how they grow, and when they die.

Acts 18:20(NASB)

"When they asked him to stay for a longer time, he did not consent, but as he left, he promised, 'I will come back if it is God's will.' Then he set sail from Ephesus."

James 4:14(NASB)

"Yet you do not know what your life will be like tomorrow. You are just a vapor that appears for a little while and then vanishes away. Instead, you ought to say, 'If the Lord wills, we will live and also do this or that.'"

Junkie Fix

What God wants He gets.

ACTS 17:5(NKJV)

"But the Jews who were not persuaded, becoming envious, took some of the evil men from the marketplace, and gathering a mob, set all the city in an uproar and attacked the house of Jason, and sought to bring them out to the people. But when they did not find them, they dragged Jason and some brethren to the rulers of the city, crying out, 'These who have turned the world upside down have come here too.'"

Junkie Fix

Can I be counted with them? Have I turned the world upside down?

ACTS 17:11(NASB)

"Now these were more noble-minded than those in Thessalonica, for they received the word with great eagerness, examining the Scriptures daily to see whether these things were so."

ISAIAH 34:16(NIV)

"Look in the scroll of the Lord and read
None of these will be missing, not one will lack her mate. For it is his mouth that has given the order, and his Spirit will gather them together."

....

....

....

....

....

....

....

....

....

....

....

....

JUNKIE FIX

....

THE BIBLE STANDS STRONG. IT'S THE WORD OF GOD FOR US.

ACTS 15:28(NIV)

"It seemed good to the Holy Spirit and to us not to burden you with anything beyond the following requirements You are to abstain from food sacrificed to idols, from blood, from the meat of strangled animals and from sexual immorality. You will do well to avoid these things. Farewell."

....

....

....

....

....

....

....

....

....

....

....

....

....

....

....

....

Junkie Fix

....

Good advice is good advice.

ACTS 15:7(NLT)

"At the meeting, after a long discussion, Peter stood and addressed them as follows "Brothers, you all know that God chose me from among you some time ago to preach to the Gentiles so that they could hear the Good News and believe."

....

....

....

....

....

....

....

....

....

....

....

....

....

....

....

....

....

JUNKIE FIX

....

PETER KNEW HIS PLACE AND I REMEMBER MINE.

LUKE 24:8(NKJV)

"And they remembered His words."

MARK 13:31(NASB)

"Heaven and earth will pass away, but My words will not pass away."

LUKE 9:44(NIV)

"Listen carefully to what I am about to tell you
The Son of Man is going to be betrayed into the hands of men."

JOHN 2:22(NKJV)

"Therefore, when He had risen from the dead, His disciples remembered that He had said this to them; and they believed the Scripture and the word which Jesus had said."

....

....

....

....

....

....

....

JUNKIE FIX

IF I DO NOT MEDITATE ON HIS WORK I WILL FORGET, I MUST FIGHT MY FLESH TO KEEP HIS WORDS IN MY HEART.

LUKE 9:45(NIV)

"But they did not understand what this meant. It was hidden from them, so that they did not grasp it, and they were afraid to ask him about it."

JUNKIE FIX

GOD IS THE TRUTH AND LIGHT HE IS THE ONLY ONE WHO WILL GIVE ME UNDERSTANDING.

LUKE 2:52(NIV)

"And Jesus grew in wisdom and stature and in favor with God and men."

Junkie Fix

Jesus grew His mind and body I must as well.

LUKE 8:52(NKJV)

"Now all wept and mourned for her; but He said, 'Do not weep; she is not dead, but sleeping.' And they ridiculed Him, knowing that she was dead."

JUNKIE FIX

DO I TRUST IN MY SENSES OR GOD? HOW DO I ACT WHEN I THINK THEY ARE DIFFERENT?

ECCLESIASTES 10:10(NASB)

"If the axe is dull and he does not sharpen its edge, then he must exert more strength. Wisdom has the advantage of giving success."

Junkie Fix

Force is not always the best answer.

ECCLESIASTES 7:10(NIV)

"Do not say, 'Why were the old days better than these?' For it is not wise to ask such questions."

JUNKIE FIX

IF I LONG FOR THE PAST, I OVERLOOK THE GOOD THAT GOD HAS DONE IN ME.

ECCLESIASTES 3:14(NASB)

"I know that everything God does will remain forever; there is nothing to add to it and there is nothing to take from it, for God has so worked that men should fear Him."

JAMES 1:17(NIV)

"Every good and perfect gift is from above, coming down from the Father of the heavenly lights, who does not change like shifting shadows."

....

....

....

....

....

....

....

....

....

....

....

....

....

JUNKIE FIX

....

KNOWING GOD AND HIS WORK IS PERFECT, BRINGS WITH IT REVERENCE AND WORSHIP.

ECCLESIASTES 12:7(NKJV)

"Then the dust will return to the earth as it was, and the spirit will return to God who gave it."

GENESIS 3:19(NASB)

"By the sweat of your face You will eat bread, Till you return to the ground, Because from it you were taken; For you are dust, And to dust you shall return."

JOB 34:14(NLT)

"If God were to take back his spirit and withdraw his breath, all life would cease, and humanity would turn again to dust."

JUNKIE FIX

MY LIFE ISN'T MINE, I DIDN'T START IT, AND GOD WILL FINISH IT.

ECCLESIASTES 1:18(NLT)

"For the greater my wisdom, the greater my grief. To increase knowledge only increases sorrow."

JUNKIE FIX

EARTHLY WISDOM AND KNOWLEDGE SUCKS BECAUSE THERE IS NO HOPE OF GOD IN IT.

Ecclesiastes 9:18(NASB)

"Wisdom is better than weapons of war, but one sinner destroys much good."

Junkie Fix

I am warned.

Proverbs 21:30(NKJV)

"There is no wisdom or understanding or counsel against the Lord."

Jeremiah 9:23(NKJV)

"Thus says the Lord 'Let not the wise man glory in his wisdom, Let not the mighty man glory in his might, Nor let the rich man glory in his riches; But let him who glories glory in this, That he understands and knows Me, That I am the Lord, exercising lovingkindness, judgment, and righteousness in the earth. For in these I delight,' says the Lord."

Acts 5:3(NKJV)

"But if it is of God, you cannot overthrow it—lest you even be found to fight against God."

1 Corinthians 3:19(NIV)

"For the wisdom of this world is foolishness in God's sight. As it is written 'He catches the wise in their craftiness'; and again, 'The Lord knows that the thoughts of the wise are futile.'"

....

....

....

....

Junkie Fix

....

God is the wisest. There is none wiser.

ECCLESIASTES 7:20(NKJV)

"For there is not a just man on earth who does good and does not sin."

1 JOHN 1:8(WEB)

"If we say that we have no sin, we deceive ourselves, and the truth is not in us."

JUNKIE FIX

WHEN I SEE OTHERS FAULTS I REMEMBER *WE ALL* SIN.

PROVERBS 19:8(NASB)

"He who gets wisdom loves his own soul; He who keeps understanding will find good."

PROVERBS 15:24(NKJV)

"The way of life winds upward for the wise that he may turn away from hell below."

PROVERBS 16:20(NASB)

"He who gives attention to the word will find good, And blessed is he who trusts in the Lord."

....

....

....

....

....

....

....

....

....

....

....

....

JUNKIE FIX

....

WISDOM AND UNDERSTANDING PROTECTS ME AND KEEPS ME IN THE BLESSINGS OF GOD.

PROVERBS 8:14(WEB)

"Counsel is mine, and sound wisdom I am understanding; I have strength."

JUNKIE FIX

THE LORD HAS AND IS EVERYTHING NEEDED TO RESIST ALL MY TEMPTATION.

PROVERBS 11:30(NKJV)

"The fruit of the righteous is a tree of life, and he who wins souls is wise."

DANIEL 12:3(NIV)

"Those who are wise will shine like the brightness of the heavens, and those who lead many to righteousness, like the stars for ever and ever."

1 CORINTHIANS 9:19(NASB)

"For though I am free from all men, I have made myself a slave to all, so that I may win more. To the Jews I became as a Jew, so that I might win Jews; to those who are under the Law, as under the Law though not being myself under the Law, so that I might win those who are under the Law; to those who are without law, as without law, though not being without the law of God but under the law of Christ, so that I might win those who are without law. To the weak, I became weak, that I might win the weak; I have become all things to all men, so that I may by all means save some."

JAMES 5:20(NKJV)

"Let him know that he who turns a sinner from the error of his way will save a soul from death and cover a multitude of sins."

....

....

....

....

Junkie Fix

Winning souls for Christ is wise and is one of the main reasons why I exist.

PROVERBS 15:31(NKJV)

"The ear that hears the rebukes of life will abide among the wise."

PROVERBS 1:7(NASB)

"The fear of the Lord is the beginning of knowledge; Fools despise wisdom and instruction."

PROVERBS 17:10(NKJV)

"Rebuke is more effective for a wise man than a hundred blows on a fool."

....

....

....

....

....

....

....

....

....

....

....

....

JUNKIE FIX

....

GETTING WISDOM MEANS I MUST BE TEACHABLE.

PROVERBS 23:4(NIV)

"Do not wear yourself out to get rich; have the wisdom to show restraint."

ECCLESIASTES 2:11(NASB)

"Thus I considered all my activities which my hands had done and the labor which I had exerted, and behold all was vanity and striving after wind and there was no profit under the sun."

MATTHEW 6:19(NKJV)

"Do not lay up for yourselves treasures on earth, where moth and rust destroy and where thieves break in and steal."

1 TIMOTHY 6:9(NLT)

"But people who long to be rich fall into temptation and are trapped by many foolish and harmful desires that plunge them into ruin and destruction. For the love of money is at the root of all kinds of evil. And some people, craving money, have wandered from the faith and pierced themselves with many sorrows."

HEBREWS 13:5(NIV)

"Keep your lives free from the love of money and be content with what you have, because God has said, 'Never will I leave you; never will I forsake you.'"

....

....

....

Junkie Fix

When I try to get wisdom rather than wealth, God will bless me.

PROVERBS 3:26(NKJV)

"For the Lord will be your confidence, and will keep your foot from being caught."

PROVERBS 3:24(NLT)

"You can lie down without fear and enjoy pleasant dreams. You need not be afraid of disaster or the destruction that comes upon the wicked."

JUNKIE FIX

GOD'S WISDOM BRINGS PEACE OF MIND AND REMOVES MY FEAR.

PROVERBS 4:23(NKJV)

"Keep your heart with all diligence, for out of it spring the issues of life."

LUKE 6:45(NKJV)

"A good man out of the good treasure of his heart brings forth good; and an evil man out of the evil treasure of his heart brings forth evil. For out of the abundance of the heart his mouth speaks."

JUNKIE FIX

I MUST BE ON GUARD AND FEED MYSELF WISDOM BECAUSE IT AFFECTS MY SPEECH AND ACTIONS.

PROVERBS 2:10(KNJV)

"When wisdom enters your heart, And knowledge is pleasant to your soul."

JUNKIE FIX

WHEN WISDOM GETS DEEP INSIDE ME, THE KNOWLEDGE IT BRINGS FILLS ME WITH JOY.

PROVERBS 3:13(NKJV)

"Happy is the man who finds wisdom, and the man who gains understanding; for her benefit is more profitable than silver, and her gain is better than gold. She is more precious than rubies, and none of the things you desire can compare with her. Long life is in her right hand; in her left hand are riches and honor. Her ways are very pleasant, and all her paths are peaceful. She is like a tree of life to those who obtain her, and everyone who grasps hold of her will be blessed."

Junkie Fix

The worth of wisdom and understanding are so great that I cannot help but be grateful.

PROVERBS 18:24(NKJV)

A man who has friends must himself be friendly, but there is a friend who sticks closer than a brother."

1 SAMUEL 18:1(NASB)

"Now it came about when he had finished speaking to Saul, that the soul of Jonathan was knit to the soul of David, and Jonathan loved him as himself."

JOHN 15:14(NKJV)

"You are My friends if you do whatever I command you. No longer do I call you servants, for a servant does not know what his master is doing; but I have called you friends, for all things that I heard from My Father I have made known to you."

....

....

....

....

....

....

....

....

JUNKIE FIX

....

FRIENDS CHOSEN WISELY ARE MORE LOYAL THAN BROTHERS.

PROVERBS 1:5(NKJV)

"A wise man will hear and increase learning, And a man of understanding will attain wise counsel."

PROVERBS 9:9(NASB)

"Give instruction to a wise man and he will be still wiser, Teach a righteous man and he will increase his learning."

....

....

....

....

....

....

....

....

....

....

....

....

....

....

....

JUNKIE FIX

....

AS A WISE BELIEVER I CAN GUIDE OTHERS WITH TRUTH.

ACTS 1:24(NASB)

"And they prayed and said, 'You, Lord, who know the hearts of all men, show which one of these two You have chosen.'"

1 SAMUEL 16:7(NIV)

"But the Lord said to Samuel, 'Do not consider his appearance or his height, for I have rejected him. The Lord does not look at the things man looks at. Man looks at the outward appearance, but the Lord looks at the heart.'"

JUNKIE FIX

I ASK GOD FOR HELP MAKING DECISIONS BECAUSE HE KNOWS EXACTLY WHAT TO LOOK FOR.

Acts 1:7(NIV)

"He said to them
'It is not for you to know the times or dates the Father has set by his own authority.'"

Matthew 24:36(KNJV)

"But of that day and hour no one knows, not even the angels of heaven, but My Father only."

Deuteronomy 29:29(NLT)

"There are secret things that belong to the Lord our God, but the revealed things belong to us and our descendants forever, so that we may obey these words of the law."

Junkie Fix

I don't know everything and that's OK. What I know I'm responsible for, what I don't is God's.

ACTS 4:21(NASB)

"When they had threatened them further, they let them go(finding no basis on which to punish them) on account of the people, because they were all glorifying God for what had happened."

MATTHEW 15:31(NKJV)

"So the multitude marveled when they saw the mute speaking, the maimed made whole, the lame walking, and the blind seeing; and they glorified the God of Israel."

JUNKIE FIX

IT'S AMAZING TO SEE WHO FEELS THREATENED BY MIRACLES BUT IT MAKES SENSE WHEN I SEE WHO IS PRAISED BY THEM.

Acts 10:38(NASB)

"You know of Jesus of Nazareth, how God anointed Him with the Holy Spirit and with power, and how He went about doing good and healing all who were oppressed by the devil, for God was with Him."

John 3:2(NKJV)

"This man came to Jesus by night and said to Him, 'Rabbi, we know that You are a teacher come from God; for no one can do these signs that You do unless God is with him.'"

John 8:29(NKJV)

"And He who sent Me is with Me. The Father has not left Me alone, for I always do those things that please Him."

Junkie Fix

Jesus is perfect.

I don't know everything. I need study but deeper than that, I need understanding to pay attention to all God says to me. Thinking about the Bible, God's words for me, is how I gain understanding. It is an oversimplification to think that every word, every sentence will give me understanding, just as if I just sit in a class, I will gain knowledge. I have to pay attention and make an effort to apply the truth that God has given me. God does not lie. He is perfect, so any fault I find must be in my perspective. Where I start, getting wisdom is being teachable. I make myself available, being open to what God has to say to me.

I am responsible for what I know; God's grace covers the rest. I can't lay back with my eyes and ears closed. God has more for me. God's wisdom is worth more than wealth. I keep His word in my heart. When I am ready to understand what He has for me, God grants me the understanding to go with it. This is why I wrote this book as I did. I can read just enough scripture, not to lose it in the business of the day. God can tell me what I need to know through it and I can write it down so I don't lose it. My hope is that others will do the same.

Heart Fixes

Issues of the heart and emotions. Love fear and all that.

ROMANS 5:3(NIV)

"Not only so, but we also rejoice in our sufferings, because we know that suffering produces perseverance; perseverance, character; and character, hope. And hope does not disappoint us, because God has poured out his love into our hearts by the Holy Spirit, whom he has given us."

JUNKIE FIX

TIMES WILL BE HARD BUT HOPE IS THERE FOR US BECAUSE GOD IS WITH US.

ROMANS 6:19(NKJV)

"I speak in human terms because of the weakness of your flesh. For just as you presented your members as slaves of uncleanness, and of lawlessness leading to more lawlessness, so now present your members as slaves of righteousness for holiness."

ROMANS 8:13(NKJV)

"For if you live according to the flesh you will die; but if by the Spirit you put to death the deeds of the body, you will live."

JUNKIE FIX

I AM NO LONGER LIVING MY LIFE BUT A BETTER LIFE, THE ONE GOD MADE FOR ME.

ROMANS 2:1(NASB)

"Therefore you have no excuse, every one of you who passes judgment, for in that which you judge another, you condemn yourself; for you who judge practice the same things."

LUKE 6:37(NIV)

"Do not judge, and you will not be judged. Do not condemn, and you will not be condemned. Forgive, and you will be forgiven."

....

....

....

....

....

....

....

....

....

....

....

....

JUNKIE FIX

....

IT'S NOT MY PLACE TO JUDGE OR CONDEMN BUT I CAN FORGIVE.

ACTS 26:28(NKJV)

"Then Agrippa said to Paul, 'You almost persuade me to become a Christian.' And Paul said, 'I would to God that not only you, but also all who hear me today, might become both almost and altogether such as I am, except for these chains.'"

....

....

....

....

....

....

....

....

....

....

....

....

....

....

....

....

Junkie Fix

....

ACTS 26:19(NASB)

"So, King Agrippa, I did not prove disobedient to the heavenly vision, but kept declaring both to those of Damascus first, and also at Jerusalem and then throughout all the region of Judea, and even to the Gentiles, that they should repent and turn to God, performing deeds appropriate to repentance."

JUNKIE FIX

WHEN MY HEART CHANGES MY ACTIONS FOLLOW.

ACTS 20:19(NIV)

"I served the Lord with great humility and with tears, although I was severely tested by the plots of the Jews. You know that I have not hesitated to preach anything that would be helpful to you but have taught you publicly and from house to house. I have declared to both Jews and Greeks that they must turn to God in repentance and have faith in our Lord Jesus."

JUNKIE FIX

SERVING GOD I TAKE THE GOOD AND THE BAD.

ACTS 26:18(NKJV)

"To open their eyes, in order to turn them from darkness to light, and from the power of Satan to God, that they may receive forgiveness of sins and an inheritance among those who are sanctified by faith in Me.'

JOHN 8:12(NASB)

"Then Jesus again spoke to them, saying, 'I am the Light of the world; he who follows Me will not walk in the darkness, but will have the Light of life.'"

....

....

....

....

....

....

....

....

....

....

....

....

....

JUNKIE FIX

....

I WANT TO REFLECT HIS LIGHT ON EARTH.

ACTS 17:16(NLT)

"While Paul was waiting for them in Athens, he was deeply troubled by all the idols he saw everywhere in the city."

2 PETER 2:8(NIV)

"For that righteous man, living among them day after day, was tormented in his righteous soul by the lawless deeds he saw and heard"

....

....

....

....

....

....

....

....

....

....

....

....

....

....

JUNKIE FIX

....

I PRAY TO BE CLOSE ENOUGH TO GOD THAT WHAT UPSETS HIM UPSETS ME DEEPLY.

ACTS 16:22(NASB)

"The crowd rose up together against them, and the chief magistrates tore their robes off them and proceeded to order them to be beaten with rods."

2CORINTHIANS 11:25(NKJV)

"Three times I was beaten with rods; once I was stoned; three times I was shipwrecked; a night and a day I have been in the deep."

1THESSALONIANS 2:2(NKJV)

"But even after we had suffered before and were spitefully treated at Philippi, as you know, we were bold in our God to speak to you the gospel of God in much conflict."

JUNKIE FIX

IT'S NOT EASY LIVING IN THE RELATIONSHIP OF CHRIST AS LORD.

ACTS 16:15(NLT)

"She was baptized along with other members of her household, and she asked us to be her guests. 'If you agree that I am faithful to the Lord,' she said, 'come and stay at my home.' And she urged us until we did."

GENESIS 19:3(NKJV)

"But he insisted strongly; so they turned in to him and entered his house. Then he made them a feast, and baked unleavened bread, and they ate."

HEBREWS 13:2(NKJV)

"Do not neglect hospitality, because through it some have entertained angels without knowing it."

....

....

....

....

....

....

....

....

....

JUNKIE FIX

....

GENEROSITY IS BEAUTIFUL.

ACTS 14:9(NASB)

"This man was listening to Paul as he spoke, who, when he had fixed his gaze on him and had seen that he had faith to be made well, said with a loud voice, 'Stand upright on your feet.' And he leaped up and began to walk."

JUNKIE FIX

I LOOK INTENTLY AT PEOPLE TO SEE WHAT GOD WILL DO THROUGH ME.

ACTS 12:23(NIV)

"Immediately, because Herod did not give praise to God, an angel of the Lord struck him down, and he was eaten by worms and died."

ROMANS 1:20(NKJV)

"For since the creation of the world His invisible attributes are clearly seen, being understood by the things that are made, even His eternal power and Godhead, so that they are without excuse, because, although they knew God, they did not glorify Him as God, nor were thankful, but became futile in their thoughts, and their foolish hearts were darkened."

JUNKIE FIX

GLORY TO GOD IS A MUST.

ACTS 13:46(NIV)

"Then Paul and Barnabas answered them boldly'We had to speak the word of God to you first. Since you reject it and do not consider yourselves worthy of eternal life, we now turn to the Gentiles.'"

MATTHEW 21:43(NKJV)

"Therefore I say to you, the kingdom of God will be taken from you and given to a nation bearing the fruits of it."

ACTS 18:5(NKJV)

"When Silas and Timothy had come from Macedonia, Paul was compelled by the Spirit, and testified to the Jews that Jesus is the Christ. But when they opposed him and blasphemed, he shook his garments and said to them, 'Your blood be upon your own heads; I am clean. From now on I will go to the Gentiles.'"

....

....

....

....

....

....

JUNKIE FIX

....

TO SHARE WITH SOMEONE AND BE REJECTED RELEASES ME OF BLAME.

LUKE 2:35(NASB)

"And a sword will pierce even your own soul—to the end that thoughts from many hearts may be revealed."

PSALM 42:10(NASB)

"As a shattering of my bones; my adversaries revile me, while they say to me all day long, 'Where is your God?'"

JUNKIE FIX

MY ACTIONS WITH OR AGAINST OTHERS REVEAL MY HEART.

Proverbs 17:3(NKJV)

"The refining pot is for silver and the furnace for gold, But the Lord tests the hearts."

1Chronicles 29:17(NKJV)

"I know also, my God, that You test the heart and have pleasure in uprightness. As for me, in the uprightness of my heart, I have willingly offered all these things; and now with joy I have seen Your people, who are present here to offer willingly to You."

Jeremiah 17:10(NIV)

"I the Lord search the heart and examine the mind, to reward a man according to his conduct, according to what his deeds deserve."

Junkie Fix

The Lord is the right tool for testing my heart.

LUKE 6:45(NKJV)

"A good man out of the good treasure of his heart brings forth good; and an evil man out of the evil treasure of his heart brings forth evil. For out of the abundance of the heart his mouth speaks."

PROVERBS 15:2(NIV)

"The tongue of the wise commends knowledge, but the mouth of the fool gushes folly."

PROVERBS 15:28(NASB)

"The heart of the righteous ponders how to answer, but the mouth of the wicked pours out evil things."

PROVERBS 18:21(NIV)

"The tongue has the power of life and death, and those who love it will eat its fruit."

JUNKIE FIX

WHEN I HAVE TO WATCH MY MOUTH, I AM NOT GUARDING MY HEART ENOUGH.

LUKE 8:14(NLT)

"The thorny ground represents those who hear and accept the message, but all too quickly the message is crowded out by the cares and riches and pleasures of this life. And so, they never grow into maturity."

ECCLESIASTES 2:11(NLT)

"But as I looked at everything I had worked so hard to accomplish, it was all so meaningless. It was like chasing the wind. There was nothing really worthwhile anywhere."

1TIMOTHY 6:9(NASB)

"But those who want to get rich fall into temptation and a snare and many foolish and harmful desires which plunge men into ruin and destruction. For the love of money is a root of all sorts of evil, and some by longing for it have wandered away from the faith and pierced themselves with many griefs."

....

....

....

....

....

JUNKIE FIX

WHEN I HEAR THE WORD OF GOD, I MUST HOLD TIGHT TO IT AND NOT LET THE CARES OF LIFE MAKE ME LOSE SIGHT OF IT.

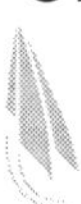

LUKE 9:62(NLT)

"But Jesus told him, 'Anyone who puts a hand to the plow and then looks back is not fit for the Kingdom of God.'"

MATTHEW 13:21(NIV)

"But since he has no root, he lasts only a short time. When trouble or persecution comes because of the word, he quickly falls away."

JAMES 4:4(NIV)

"You adulterous people, don't you know that friendship with the world is hatred towards God? Anyone who chooses to be a friend of the world becomes an enemy of God."

1 JOHN 2:15(NASB)

"Do not love the world nor the things in the world. If anyone loves the world, the love of the Father is not in him. For all that is in the world, the lust of the flesh and the lust of the eyes and the boastful pride of life, is not from the Father, but is from the world. The world is passing away, and also its lusts; but the one who does the will of God lives forever."

Junkie Fix

Work for the Lord must be whole hearted.

LUKE 20:18(NIV)

"Everyone who falls on that stone will be broken to pieces, but he on whom it falls will be crushed."

DANIEL 2:44(NLT)

"During the reigns of those kings, the God of heaven will set up a kingdom that will never be destroyed; no one will ever conquer it. It will shatter all these kingdoms into nothingness, but it will stand forever. That is the meaning of the rock cut from the mountain by supernatural means, crushing to dust the statue of iron, bronze, clay, silver, and gold. 'The great God has shown Your Majesty what will happen in the future. The dream is true, and its meaning is certain.'"

JUNKIE FIX

I FEEL BROKEN OFTEN, BUT NOT CRUSHED. GOD'S KINGDOM SHALL REIGN FOREVER; NO CHALLENGERS CAN STAND AGAINST GOD'S WRATH.

LUKE 22:62(NKJV)

"So Peter went out and wept bitterly."

LUKE 7:38(NKJV)

"And stood at His feet behind Him weeping; and she began to wash His feet with her tears, and wiped them with the hair of her head; and she kissed His feet and anointed them with the fragrant oil."

LUKE 18:13(NASB)

"But the tax collector, standing some distance away, was even unwilling to lift up his eyes to heaven, but was beating his breast, saying, 'God, be merciful to me, the sinner!'"

JUNKIE FIX

CRYING IS AGREEING WITH GOD ON HOW AWFUL SIN IS, MIXED WITH THE KNOWLEDGE THAT I SINNED AGAINST HIM.

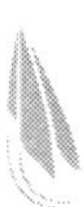

LUKE 5:8(NLT)

"When Simon Peter realized what had happened, he fell to his knees before Jesus and said, 'Oh, Lord, please leave me--I'm too much of a sinner to be around you.'"

JUNKIE FIX

WHEN I AM CONFRONTED WITH THE POWER OF GOD, I AM CONVICTED OF MY OWN UNWORTHINESS.

LUKE 22:44(NKJV)

"And being in agony, He prayed more earnestly. Then His sweat became like great drops of blood falling down to the ground."

Junkie Fix

Now this is prayer, passionate and sincere.

LUKE 18:13(NKJV)

"And the tax collector, standing afar off, would not so much as raise his eyes to heaven, but beat his breast, saying, 'God, be merciful to me a sinner!'"

1 PETER 5:5(NLT)

"You younger men, accept the authority of the elders. And all of you serve each other in humility, for 'God sets himself against the proud, but he shows favor to the humble.'"

....

....

....

....

....

....

....

....

....

....

....

....

....

JUNKIE FIX

....

THIS IS HOW I WANT TO KEEP MY HEART.

MARK 10:49(NIV)

"Jesus stopped and said, 'Call him.' So they called to the blind man, 'Cheer up! On your feet! He's calling you.'"

JUNKIE FIX

JESUS HEARS ME WHEN I CRY OUT. MY HEART MUST BECOME RIGHT BEFORE HE ASKS ME TO DO WHATEVER HE WILLS. HE LOVES ME AND MEETS ME WHERE I AM. HE WORKS WITH ME TO GET ME WHERE HE WANTS ME.

MARK 9:40(NLT)

"Anyone who is not against us is for us."

LUKE 11:23(NKJV)

"He who is not with Me is against Me, and he who does not gather with Me scatters."

JUNKIE FIX

IF SOMEONE DOES GOOD IN CHRIST'S NAME, THEY ARE ON MY SIDE.

Luke 12:2(NASB)

"But there is nothing covered up that will not be revealed, and hidden that will not be known."

Matthew 10:34(NLT)

"Don't imagine that I came to bring peace to the earth! No, I came to bring a sword. I have come to set a man against his father, and a daughter against her mother, and a daughter-in-law against her mother-in-law. Your enemies will be right in your own household!"

John 7:43(NKJV)

"So there was a division among the people because of Him."

Acts 14:4(NIV)

"The people of the city were divided; some sided with the Jews, others with the apostles."

....

....

....

....

....

....

Junkie Fix

FIRE FROM GOD IS CONSUMING AND PASSIONATE. THE ONES ON FIRE WILL BE DIVIDED FROM THOSE WHO AREN'T.

LUKE 17:4(NLT)

"Even if he wrongs you seven times a day and each time turns again and asks forgiveness, forgive him."

EPHESIANS 4:32(NASB)

"Be kind to one another, tenderhearted, forgiving each other, just as God in Christ also has forgiven you."

COLOSSIANS 3:13(NKJV)

"Bearing with one another, and forgiving one another, if anyone has a complaint against another; even as Christ forgave you, so you also must do."

JUNKIE FIX

I MUST FORGIVE BEYOND WHAT I THINK I CAN BEAR, THAT'S WHAT GOD ASKS OF ME. GOD FORGIVES EVEN MORE THAN I ASK.

PROVERBS 3:3(NASB)

"Do not let kindness and truth leave you; Bind them around your neck, Write them on the tablet of your heart."

2CORINTHIANS 3:3(NLT)

"Clearly, you are a letter from Christ prepared by us. It is written not with pen and ink, but with the Spirit of the living God. It is carved not on stone, but on human hearts."

JUNKIE FIX

I MUST STRIVE TO KEEP THE MERCY AND TRUTH THAT COMES FROM GOD IN ME TO PROTECT ME FROM MY SINFUL DESIRES.

PROVERBS 11:25(NKJV)

"The generous soul will be made rich, and he who waters will also be watered himself."

2CORINTHIANS 9:6(NLT)

"Remember this--a farmer who plants only a few seeds will get a small crop. But the one who plants generously will get a generous crop. You must each make up your own mind as to how much you should give. Don't give reluctantly or in response to pressure. For God loves the person who gives cheerfully."

MATTHEW 5:7(NASB)

"Blessed are the merciful, for they shall receive mercy. Blessed are the pure in heart, for they shall see God."

JUNKIE FIX

GOD KNOWS MY HEART. GIVE AND GOD GIVES BACK.

PROVERBS 1:7(NASB)

"The fear of the Lord is the beginning of knowledge. Fools despise wisdom and instruction."

JOB 28:28(NLT)

"And this is what he says to all humanity
'The fear of the Lord is true wisdom; to forsake evil is real understanding.'"

ECCLESIASTES 12:13(NIV)

"Now all has been heard; here is the conclusion of the matter Fear God and keep his commandments, for this is the whole duty of man."

PSALM 42:1(NIV)

"As the deer pants for streams of water, so my soul pants for you, O God."

JUNKIE FIX

FEARING THE LORD IS THE BEGINNING; GOD IS GOOD SO FOLLOWING HIM WILL MAKE ME STOP DOING EVIL. THIS SHOULD BE A LONGING OF MY HEART TO KNOW AND BE MORE LIKE GOD.

PROVERBS 30:5(WEB)

"Every word of God is pure
he is a shield to them that put their trust in him."

2SAMUEL 22:31(NKJV)

"As for God, His way is perfect; The word of the Lord is proven; He is a shield to all who trust in Him."

JUNKIE FIX

THE BIBLE IS PROTECTION FOR ME BECAUSE I TRUST IN GOD.

PROVERBS 10:12(NKJV)

"Hatred stirs up strife, but love covers all sins."

1 CORINTHIANS 13:4(NIV)

"Love is patient, love is kind. It does not envy, it does not boast, it is not proud. It is not rude, it is not self-seeking, it is not easily angered, it keeps no record of wrongs. Love does not delight in evil but rejoices with the truth. It always protects, always trusts, always hopes, always perseveres. Love never fails. But where there are prophecies, they will cease; where there are tongues, they will be stilled; where there is knowledge, it will pass away."

JAMES 5:20(NIV)

"Remember this Whoever turns a sinner from the error of his way will save him from death and cover over a multitude of sins."

1 PETER 4:8(NIV)

"Above all, love each other deeply, because love covers over a multitude of sins."

....

....

....

....

JUNKIE FIX

....

TRUE LOVE, WHICH IS GOD'S LOVE, STRUGGLES FOR THE GREATEST GOOD FOR ME.

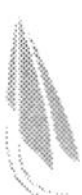

PROVERBS 6:23(NIV)

"For these commands are a lamp, this teaching is a light, and the corrections of discipline are the way to life."

2 PETER 1:19(NLT)

"Because of that, we have even greater confidence in the message proclaimed by the prophets. Pay close attention to what they wrote, for their words are like a light shining in a dark place--until the day Christ appears and his brilliant light shines in your hearts."

JUNKIE FIX

THE WORD OF GOD REVEALS THE FLAWED PARTS OF MY HEART TO CORRECT ME, SO THAT I CAN HAVE AN ABUNDANT AND ETERNAL LIFE.

PROVERBS 9:8(NKJV)

"Do not correct a scoffer, lest he hate you; Rebuke a wise man, and he will love you."

PSALM 141:5(NKJV)

"Let the righteous strike me; It shall be a kindness. And let him rebuke me; It shall be as excellent oil; Let my head not refuse it."

MATTHEW 13:12(NKJV)

"For whoever has, to him more will be given, and he will have abundance; but whoever does not have, even what he has will be taken away from him."

....

....

....

....

....

....

....

....

....

....

JUNKIE FIX

....

WHEN I AM CORRECTED, I AM THANKFUL THAT I CAN BECOME A BETTER PERSON BY CHANGING, INSTEAD OF HATING THE PERSON WHO CARES ENOUGH TO TELL ME.

PROVERBS 17:17(NKJV)

"A friend loves at all times, And a brother is born for adversity."

RUTH 1:16(NLT)

"But Ruth replied, 'Don't ask me to leave you and turn back. I will go wherever you go and live wherever you live. Your people will be my people, and your God will be my God.'"

PROVERBS 18:24(NKJV)

"A man who has friends must himself be friendly, But there is a friend who sticks closer than a brother."

....

....

....

....

....

....

....

....

....

....

JUNKIE FIX

....

MY TRUE FRIEND LOVES ALWAYS.

PROVERBS 14:10(NLT)

"Each heart knows its own bitterness, and no one else can fully share its joy."

1 KINGS 8:28(NIV)

"Yet give attention to your servant's prayer and his plea for mercy, O Lord my God. Hear the cry and the prayer that your servant is praying in your presence this day."

MATTHEW 26:39(NKJV)

"He went a little farther and fell on His face, and prayed, saying, 'O My Father, if it is possible, let this cup pass from Me; nevertheless, not as I will, but as You will.' Then He came to the disciples and found them sleeping, and said to Peter, 'What! Could you not watch with Me one hour? Watch and pray, lest you enter into temptation. The spirit indeed is willing, but the flesh is weak.' Again, a second time, He went away and prayed, saying, 'O My Father, if this cup cannot pass away from Me unless I drink it, Your will be done.'"

JUNKIE FIX

PAIN AND JOY ARE PERSONAL. ONLY GOD KNOWS. NO OTHER PERSON CAN UNDERSTAND THEM THE WAY I DO.

PROVERBS 29:25(NKJV)

"The fear of man brings a snare, But whoever trusts in the Lord shall be safe."

LUKE 12:4(NLT)

"Dear friends, don't be afraid of those who want to kill you. They can only kill the body; they cannot do any more to you."

JOHN 12:42(NKJV)

"Nevertheless even among the rulers many believed in Him, but because of the Pharisees they did not confess Him, lest they should be put out of the synagogue; for they loved the praise of men more than the praise of God."

JUNKIE FIX

I WILL FEAR THE LORD MOST, AND THE FEAR OF MAN WILL NOT KEEP ME FROM HIM.

PROVERBS 19:11(NASB)

"A man's discretion makes him slow to anger, And it is his glory to overlook a transgression."

MATTHEW 5:44(NKJV)

"But I say to you, love your enemies, bless those who curse you, do good to those who hate you, and pray for those who spitefully use you and persecute you."

EPHESIANS 4:32(NASB)

"Be kind to one another, tender-hearted, forgiving each other, just as God in Christ also has forgiven you."

COLOSSIANS 3:13(NIV)

"Bear with each other and forgive whatever grievances you may have against one another. Forgive as the Lord forgave you."

JOHN 16:24(NASB)

"Until now you have asked for nothing in My name; ask and you will receive, so that your joy may be made full."

JAMES 1:19(NLT)

"My dear brothers and sisters, be quick to listen, slow to speak, and slow to get angry."

....

....

....

Junkie Fix

Love others. With Christ, I can forgive even my enemy.

Proverbs 12:25(NASB)

"Anxiety in a man's heart weighs it down, but a good word makes it glad."

Isaiah 50:4(NKJV)

"The Lord God has given Me The tongue of the learned, That I should know how to speak A word in season to him who is weary. He awakens Me morning by morning; He awakens My ear To hear as the learned."

Junkie Fix

God has given me words to lift up others. I am valued by God.

PROVERBS 19:22(NKJV)

"What is desired in a man is kindness, and a poor man is better than a liar."

PROVERBS 28:6(NIV)

"Better a poor man whose walk is blameless than a rich man whose ways are perverse."

JUNKIE FIX

RICH OR POOR, GOODNESS IS WHAT MATTERS.

PROVERBS 1:19(NLT)

"Such is the fate of all who are greedy for gain. It ends up robbing them of life."

1TIMOTHY 6:10(NKJV)

"For the love of money is a root of all kinds of evil, for which some have strayed from the faith in their greediness, and pierced themselves through with many sorrows."

JUNKIE FIX

GOD DID NOT CREATE ME SO THAT I COULD BE RICH, THAT LONGING TAKES ME AWAY FROM GOD.

ECCLESIASTES 2:11(NKJV)

"Then I looked on all the works that my hands had done And on the labor in which I had toiled; And indeed all was vanity and grasping for the wind. There was no profit under the sun."

LUKE 8:14(NKJV)

"Now the ones that fell among thorns are those who, when they have heard, go out and are choked with cares, riches, and pleasures of life, and bring no fruit to maturity."

JUNKIE FIX

EARTHLY PLEASURE IS NOT AUTOMATICALLY EVIL, JUST FRUITLESS. THE POINTLESSNESS OF LABOR IS THAT NOTHING LASTING COMES FROM IT.

PROVERBS 10:22(NASB)

"It is the blessing of the Lord that makes riches, And He adds no sorrow to it."

Junkie Fix

The guilt that comes from sinful profit doesn't come from the valuables given by God.

MARK 10:24(NASB)

"The disciples were amazed at His words. But Jesus answered again and said to them, 'Children, how hard it is to enter the kingdom of God! It is easier for a camel to go through the eye of a needle than for a rich man to enter the kingdom of God.'"

PSALM 62:10(NIV)

"Do not trust in extortion or take pride in stolen goods; though your riches increase, do not set your heart on them."

1TIMOTHY 6:17(NIV)

"Command those who are rich in this present world not to be arrogant nor to put their hope in wealth, which is so uncertain, but to put their hope in God, who richly provides us with everything for our enjoyment."

....

....

....

....

....

....

....

JUNKIE FIX

IT IS IMPOSSIBLE TO ENTER HEAVEN EXCEPT BY CHRIST WHO WANTS MY HEART TO BE LIKE A TRUSTING TODDLER. THIS PART SPEAKS OF THE HEART NOT THE WALLET.

Luke 6:30(NLT)

"Give what you have to anyone who asks you for it; and when things are taken away from you, don't try to get them back."

Deuteronomy 15:7(NKJV)

"If there is among you a poor man of your brethren, within any of the gates in your land which the Lord your God is giving you, you shall not harden your heart nor shut your hand from your poor brother, but you shall open your hand wide to him and willingly lend him sufficient for his need, whatever he needs."

Proverbs 21:26(NASB)

"All day long he is craving, While the righteous gives and does not hold back."

Hebrews 13:16(NKJV)

"But do not forget to do good and to share, for with such sacrifices God is well pleased."

....

....

....

....

Junkie Fix

....

Generosity showing my heart is not bound to the earth.

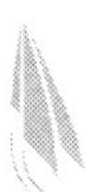

ECCLESIASTES 7:14(NLT)

"Enjoy prosperity while you can. But when hard times strike, realize that both come from God. That way you will realize that nothing is certain in this life."

JUNKIE FIX

GOD MAKES THE GOOD AND BAD DAYS, I TAKE JOY THAT GOD IS IN CONTROL.

LUKE 16:15(NKJV)

"And He said to them, 'You are those who justify yourselves before men, but God knows your hearts. For what is highly esteemed among men is an abomination in the sight of God.'"

1 SAMUEL 16:7(NIV)

"But the Lord said to Samuel, 'Do not consider his appearance or his height, for I have rejected him. The Lord does not look at the things man looks at. Man looks at the outward appearance, but the Lord looks at the heart."

1 CHRONICLES 28:9(NKJV)

"As for you, my son Solomon, know the God of your father, and serve Him with a loyal heart and with a willing mind; for the Lord searches all hearts and understands all the intent of the thoughts. If you seek Him, He will be found by you; but if you forsake Him, He will cast you off forever."

PSALM 7:9(NKJV)

"Oh, let the wickedness of the wicked come to an end, But establish the just; For the righteous God tests the hearts and minds."

PROVERBS 16:5(NKJV)

"Everyone proud in heart is an abomination to the Lord; Though they join forces, none will go unpunished."

JUNKIE FIX

I WILL NOT LIFT MYSELF UP IN THIS LIFE. MY HEART MUST BE KEPT PURE TO SERVE GOD.

LUKE 14:11(NASB)

"For everyone who exalts himself will be humbled, and he who humbles himself will be exalted."

JOB 22:29(NKJV)

"When they cast you down, and you say, 'Exaltation will come!' Then He will save the humble person."

PSALM 18:27(NLT)

"You rescue those who are humble, but you humiliate the proud."

PROVERBS 29:23(NKJV)

" A man's pride will bring him low, But the humble in spirit will retain honor."

LUKE 18:14(NKJV)

"I tell you, this man went down to his house justified rather than the other; for everyone who exalts himself will be humbled, and he who humbles himself will be exalted."

....

....

....

....

JUNKIE FIX

....

ONCE AGAIN GOD WORKS OPPOSITE THAN MAN, HUMILITY BRINGS HONORS.

LUKE 15:18(NIV)

"I will set out and go back to my father and say to him Father, I have sinned against heaven and against you."

EXODUS 9:27(NASB)

"Then Pharaoh sent for Moses and Aaron, and said to them, 'I have sinned this time; the Lord is the righteous one, and I and my people are the wicked ones.'"

1 SAMUEL 15:24(NKJV)

Then Saul said to Samuel, 'I have sinned, for I have transgressed the commandment of the Lord and your words, because I feared the people and obeyed their voice.'"

1 SAMUEL 26:21(NLT)

"Then Saul confessed, 'I have sinned. Come back home, my son, and I will no longer try to harm you, for you valued my life today. I have been a fool and very, very wrong.'"

2 SAMUEL 24:10(NLT)

"But after he had taken the census, David's conscience began to bother him. And he said to the Lord, 'I have sinned greatly and shouldn't have taken the census. Please forgive me, Lord, for doing this foolish thing.'"

PSALM 51:4(NKJV)

"Against You, You only, have I sinned, And done this evil in Your sight—That You may be found just when You speak, And blameless when You judge."

Junkie Fix

I must humble myself and ask forgiveness of others, being sincere, humble, and expecting nothing.

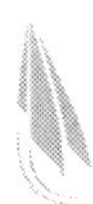

LUKE 14:26(NKJV)

"If anyone comes to Me and does not hate his father and mother, wife and children, brothers and sisters, yes, and his own life also, he cannot be My disciple."

DEUTERONOMY 13:6(NKJV)

"If your brother, the son of your mother, your son or your daughter, the wife of your bosom, or your friend who is as your own soul, secretly entices you, saying, 'Let us go and serve other gods,' which you have not known, neither you nor your fathers."

MATTHEW 10:37(NKJV)

"He who loves father or mother more than Me is not worthy of Me. And he who loves son or daughter more than Me is not worthy of Me."

REVELATIONS 12:11(NIV)

"They overcame him by the blood of the Lamb and by the word of their testimony; they did not love their lives so much as to shrink from death."

....

....

....

....

....

....

....

....

....

Junkie Fix

Love for God must come first.

LUKE 6:35(NLT)

"Love your enemies! Do good to them! Lend to them! And don't be concerned that they might not repay. Then your reward from heaven will be very great, and you will truly be acting as children of the Most High, for he is kind to the unthankful and to those who are wicked."

ROMANS 13:10(NASB)

"Love does no wrong to a neighbor; therefore, love is the fulfillment of the law."

JUNKIE FIX

GOD CALLS ME TO LOVE AS HE DID.

LUKE 22:32(NKJV)

"But I have prayed for you, that your faith should not fail; and when you have returned to Me, strengthen your brethren."

JOHN 17:15(NKJV)

"I do not pray that You should take them out of the world, but that You should keep them from the evil one."

JOHN 21:15(NKJV)

"So when they had eaten breakfast, Jesus said to Simon Peter, 'Simon, son of Jonah, do you love Me more than these?' He said to Him, 'Yes, Lord; You know that I love You.' He said to him, 'Feed My lambs.' He said to him again a second time, 'Simon, son of Jonah, do you love Me?' He said to Him, 'Yes, Lord; You know that I love You.' He said to him, 'Tend My sheep.' He said to him the third time, "Simon, son of Jonah, do you love Me?" Peter was grieved because He said to him the third time, 'Do you love Me?' And he said to Him, 'Lord, You know all things; You know that I love You.' Jesus said to him, 'Feed My sheep.'"

2 PETER 1:10(NKJV)

"Therefore, brethren, be even more diligent to make your call and election sure, for if you do these things you will never stumble; for so an entrance will be supplied to you abundantly into the everlasting kingdom of our Lord and Savior Jesus Christ. For this reason I will not be negligent to remind you always of these things, though you know and are established in the present truth. Yes, I think it is right, as long as I am in this tent, to stir you

up by reminding you, knowing that shortly I must put off my tent, just as our Lord Jesus Christ showed me. Moreover, I will be careful to ensure that you always have a reminder of these things after my decease."

JUNKIE FIX

GOD MAKES IT CLEAR TO ME, ENCOURAGE MY FAMILY IN CHRIST.

LUKE 10:21(NLT)

"Then Jesus was filled with the joy of the Holy Spirit and said, 'O Father, Lord of heaven and earth, thank you for hiding the truth from those who think themselves so wise and clever, and for revealing it to the childlike. Yes, Father, it pleased you to do it this way.'"

MARK 9:37(NKJV)

"Whoever receives one of these little children in My name receives Me; and whoever receives Me, receives not Me but Him who sent Me."

JUNKIE FIX

JESUS THANKED GOD THAT HE USED PEOPLE WITH HEARTS LIKE CHILDREN INSTEAD OF SELF-RIGHTEOUS OR CORRUPT PEOPLE.

LUKE 20:36(NASB)

"For they cannot even die anymore, because they are like angels, and are sons of God, being sons of the resurrection."

1 CORINTHIANS 15:52(NLT)

"It will happen in a moment, in the blinking of an eye, when the last trumpet is blown. For when the trumpet sounds, the Christians who have died will be raised with transformed bodies. And then we who are living will be transformed so that we will never die."

1 JOHN 3:2(NASB)

"Beloved, now we are children of God, and it has not appeared as yet what we will be. We know that when He appears, we will be like Him, because we will see Him just as He is."

....

....

....

....

....

....

....

JUNKIE FIX

....

I LONG TO BE CLEANSED OF THIS LIFE,
BECOMING A SON OF THE RESURRECTION.

ACTS 2:43(NKJV)

"Then fear came upon every soul, and many wonders and signs were done through the apostles."

MALACHI 3:16(NKJV)

"Then those who feared the Lord spoke to one another, And the Lord listened and heard them; So a book of remembrance was written before Him For those who fear the Lord And who meditate on His name. 'They shall be Mine,' says the Lord of hosts, 'On the day that I make them My jewels. And I will spare them as a man spares his own son who serves him.'"

JUNKIE FIX

FEAR OF GOD IS IMPORTANT TO ME.

ECCLESIASTES 12:13(NIV)

"Now all has been heard; here is the conclusion of the matter Fear God and keep his commandments, for this is the whole duty of man."

DEUTERONOMY 10:12(NASB)

"Now, Israel, what does the Lord your God require from you, but to fear the Lord your God, to walk in all His ways and love Him, and to serve the Lord your God with all your heart and with all your soul."

MICAH 6:8(NASB)

"He has told you, O man, what is good; And what does the Lord require of you But to do justice, to love kindness, And to walk humbly with your God?"

....

....

....

....

....

....

....

....

JUNKIE FIX

....

I MUST FOCUS ON MY RELATIONSHIP WITH GOD.

Acts 2:46(NASB)

"Day by day continuing with one mind in the temple, and breaking bread from house to house, they were taking their meals together with gladness and sincerity of heart."

Luke 24:30(NKJV)

"Now it came to pass, as He sat at the table with them, that He took bread, blessed and broke it, and gave it to them."

Acts 2:42(NIV)

"They devoted themselves to the apostles' teaching and to the fellowship, to the breaking of bread and to prayer."

Acts 20:7(NASB)

"On the first day of the week, when we were gathered together to break bread, Paul began talking to them, intending to leave the next day, and he prolonged his message until midnight."

Junkie Fix

Simplicity of heart. I like to eat and worship, simple.

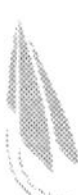

ACTS 2:47(NASB)

"Praising God and having favor with all the people. And the Lord was adding to their number day by day those who were being saved."

ACTS 5:14(NLT)

"And more and more people believed and were brought to the Lord--crowds of both men and women."

ACTS 11:21(NIV)

"The Lord's hand was with them, and a great number of people believed and turned to the Lord."

JUNKIE FIX

I LOVE MY FAMILY AND THERE IS ALWAYS ROOM FOR MORE.

ACTS 4:32(NIV)

"All the believers were one in heart and mind. No one claimed that any of his possessions was his own, but they shared everything they had. With great power, the apostles continued to testify to the resurrection of the Lord Jesus, and much grace was upon them all. There were no needy persons among them. For from time to time those who owned lands or houses sold them, brought the money from the sales and put it at the apostles' feet, and it was distributed to anyone as he had need."

Junkie Fix

Wow, I want to live there.

Acts 3:7(NLT)

"Then Peter took the lame man by the right hand and helped him up. And as he did, the man's feet and anklebones were healed and strengthened. He jumped up, stood on his feet, and began to walk! Then, walking, leaping, and praising God, he went into the Temple with them."

Isaiah 35:6(NIV)

"Then will the lame leap like a deer, and the mute tongue shout for joy. Water will gush forth in the wilderness and streams in the desert."

Junkie Fix

Beautiful is... joy bursting out.

ACTS 9:13(NKJV)

"Then Ananias answered, 'Lord, I have heard from many about this man, how much harm he has done to Your saints in Jerusalem. And here he has authority from the chief priests to bind all who call on Your name.' But the Lord said to him, 'Go, for he is a chosen vessel of Mine to bear My name before Gentiles, kings, and the children of Israel. For I will show him how many things he must suffer for My name's sake.'"

JUNKIE FIX

GOD CAN USE ANYONE HE WANTS.

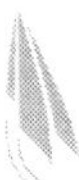

ACTS 5:40(NASB)

"They took his advice; and after calling the apostles in, they flogged them and ordered them not to speak in the name of Jesus, and then released them. So, they went on their way from the presence of the Council, rejoicing that they had been considered worthy to suffer shame for His name. And every day, in the temple and from house to house, they kept right on teaching and preaching Jesus as the Christ."

1 PETER 4:13(NKJV)

"But rejoice to the extent that you partake of Christ's sufferings, that when His glory is revealed, you may also be glad with exceeding joy. If you are reproached for the name of Christ, blessed are you, for the Spirit of glory and of God rests upon you. On their part, He is blasphemed, but on your part, He is glorified."

....

....

....

....

....

....

....

JUNKIE FIX

....

AM I WORTHY TO SUFFER SHAME?

ACTS 9:21(NKJV)

"Then all who heard were amazed, and said, 'Is this not he who destroyed those who called on this name in Jerusalem, and has come here for that purpose, so that he might bring them bound to the chief priests?' But Saul increased all the more in strength, and confounded the Jews who dwelt in Damascus, proving that this Jesus is the Christ."

JUNKIE FIX

THIS IS A GOOD REMINDER FOR ME WHEN I FEEL UNWORTHY TO BE USED BY GOD.

Love, hope, forgiveness, compassion, glory to God, sincerity, mercy, truth, fear of the Lord, thankfulness, trust, joy, generosity, purity, humility, and simplicity all things. I must keep these in my heart but they can be in short supply from time to time. God reminds me how important my heart is in our relationship, and in my relationship with everyone else. If I go through the motions, I am constantly reminded that's not good enough.

I must forgive beyond what I think I can bear because I was forgiven even more. I give glory to God that He repaired our relationship. My heart changing altered my actions. Now when I find what upsets God, I am upset too.

Bible Junkie Hard Core Challenge:

Tell

This is where it gets hard. Bible Junkies separate yourselves from wannabes Speak up and be heard.

ACTS 26:22(NKJV)

"Therefore, having obtained help from God, to this day I stand, witnessing both to small and great, saying no other things than those which the prophets and Moses said would come-- that the Christ would suffer, that He would be the first to rise from the dead, and would proclaim light to the Jewish people and to the Gentiles."

JUNKIE FIX

GOD HELPS ME SAY WHAT HE WANTS SAID.

ACTS 20:26(NASB)

"Therefore, I testify to you this day that I am innocent of the blood of all men. For I did not shrink from declaring to you the whole purpose of God. Be on guard for yourselves and for all the flock, among which the Holy Spirit has made you overseers, to shepherd the church of God which He purchased with His own blood.

JUNKIE FIX

I NEED TO SHARE MORE.

ACTS 14:22(NLT)

"Be on guard for yourselves and for all the flock, among which the Holy Spirit has made you overseers, to shepherd the church of God which He purchased with His own blood."

ACTS 11:23(NLT)

"When he arrived and saw this proof of God's favor, he was filled with joy, and he encouraged the believers to stay true to the Lord."

ROMANS 8:17(NIV)

"Now if we are children, then we are heirs—heirs of God and co-heirs with Christ, if indeed we share in his sufferings in order that we may also share in his glory."

....

....

....

....

....

....

....

....

JUNKIE FIX

I SAY TO EVERYONE DOING GOD'S WILL, "KEEP IT UP, IT'S NOT EASY, BUT IT IS WORTH IT."

ACTS 14:27(NASB)

"When they had arrived and gathered the church together, they began to report all things that God had done with them and how He had opened a door of faith to the Gentiles."

JUNKIE FIX

IT IS AWESOME TO HEAR VICTORIES FROM THE FAITHFUL.

LUKE 12:8(NET)

"I tell you, whoever acknowledges me before men, the Son of Man will also acknowledge before God's angels."

1 SAMUEL 2:30(NLT)

"Therefore, the Lord, the God of Israel, says The terrible things you are doing cannot continue! I had promised that your branch of the tribe of Levi would always be my priests. But I will honor only those who honor me, and I will despise those who despise me."

PSALM 119:46(NKJV)

"I will speak of Your testimonies also before kings, And will not be ashamed."

MATTHEW 10:32(NKJV)

"Therefore whoever confesses Me before men, him I will also confess before My Father who is in heaven."

MARK 8:38(NKJV)

"For whoever is ashamed of Me and My words in this adulterous and sinful generation, of him the Son of Man also will be ashamed when He comes in the glory of His Father with the holy angels."

ROMANS 10:9(NKJV)

"That if you confess with your mouth the Lord Jesus and believe in your heart that God has raised Him from the dead, you will be saved."

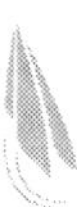

2 Timothy 2:12 (NKJV)

"If we endure, We shall also reign with Him. If we deny Him, He also will deny us."

1 John 2:23 (NASB)

"Whoever denies the Son does not have the Father; the one who confesses the Son has the Father also."

Junkie Fix

I tell all about God.

LUKE 9:20(NKJV)

"He said to them, 'But who do you say that I am?' Peter answered and said, 'The Christ of God.'"

MATTHEW 16:16(NKJV)

"Simon Peter answered and said, 'You are the Christ, the Son of the living God.'"

JOHN 6:68(NKJV)

"But Simon Peter answered Him, 'Lord, to whom shall we go? You have the words of eternal life. Also we have come to believe and know that You are the Christ, the Son of the living God.'"

JUNKIE FIX

WHO DO I SAY JESUS IS? DO I HAVE TO BE ASKED BEFORE I TELL THEM?

MARK 16:20(NIV)

"Then the disciples went out and preached everywhere, and the Lord worked with them and confirmed his word by the signs that accompanied it."

1 CORINTHIANS 2:4(NIV)

"My message and my preaching were not with wise and persuasive words, but with a demonstration of the Spirit's power,"

HEBREWS 2:4(NASB)

"God also testifying with them, both by signs and wonders and by various miracles and by gifts of the Holy Spirit according to His own will."

....

....

....

....

....

....

....

....

....

JUNKIE FIX

....

SPEAK AND GOD WILL DO THE REST.

LUKE 11:20(WEB)

"But if I with the finger of God cast out demons, no doubt the kingdom of God is come upon you."

EXODUS 8:19(NKJV)

"Then the magicians said to Pharaoh, 'This is the finger of God.' But Pharaoh's heart grew hard, and he did not heed them, just as the Lord had said."

JUNKIE FIX

WHEN GOD WORKS IN MY LIFE I MUST SAY HIS POWER IS HERE.

LUKE 10:9(NIV)

"Heal the sick who are there and tell them, 'The kingdom of God is near you.'"

MATTHEW 3:2(NKJV)

"Repent, for the kingdom of heaven is at hand!"

JUNKIE FIX

TELL OTHERS HE IS COMING.

LUKE 19:27(NIV)

"But those enemies of mine who did not want me to be a king over them—bring them here and kill them in front of me."

REVELATIONS 19:20(NASB)

"And the beast was seized, and with him the false prophet who performed the signs in his presence, by which he deceived those who had received the mark of the beast and those who worshiped his image; these two were thrown alive into the lake of fire which burns with brimstone."

....

....

....

....

....

....

....

....

....

....

....

JUNKIE FIX

....

CHRIST IS MUCH TOUGHER THAN I WAS TOLD. HE IS JUST.

PROVERBS 25:25(NIV)

"Like cold water to a weary soul is good news from a distant land."

PROVERBS 15:30(NKJV)

"The light of the eyes rejoices the heart, And a good report makes the bones healthy."

....

....

....

....

....

....

....

....

....

....

....

....

....

....

....

JUNKIE FIX

....

I WILL SHARE GOOD NEWS WITH EVERYONE EVEN THE DISTANT FRIENDS.

PROVERBS 17:10(NKJV)

"Rebuke is more effective for a wise man Than a hundred blows on a fool."

MICAH 7:9(NLT)

"I will be patient as the Lord punishes me, for I have sinned against him. But after that, he will take up my case and punish my enemies for all the evil they have done to me. The Lord will bring me out of my darkness into the light, and I will see his righteousness."

....

....

....

....

....

....

....

....

....

....

....

....

....

JUNKIE FIX

....

I AM NOT CALLED TO DELIVER THE BLOWS TO THE FOOL.

PROVERBS 27:5(NASB)

"Better is open rebuke than love that is concealed."

GALATIANS 2:14(NKJV)

"But when I saw that they were not straightforward about the truth of the gospel, I said to Peter before them all, 'If you, being a Jew, live in the manner of Gentiles and not as the Jews, why do you compel Gentiles to live as Jews?'"

JUNKIE FIX

TRUE LOVE BRINGS WITH IT TRUTH, EVEN WHEN IT MEANS A REBUKE.

MARK 1:22(NKJV)

"And they were astonished at His teaching, for He taught them as one having authority, and not as the scribes."

JUNKIE FIX

JESUS TAUGHT DIRECTLY, PERSONALLY, AND FORCEFULLY, AS MY TEACHINGS SHOULD BE.

LUKE 8:3 9(NASB)

"'Return to your house and describe what great things God has done for you.' So he went away, proclaiming throughout the whole city what great things Jesus had done for him."

JUNKIE FIX

I MUST TESTIFY, BOLDLY, CRYING OUT GOD'S WORK IN ME.

LUKE 1:49(NKJV)

"For He who is mighty has done great things for me, And holy is His name."

PSALM 126:2(NKJV)

"Then our mouth was filled with laughter, And our tongue with singing. Then they said among the nations, 'The Lord has done great things for them. The Lord has done great things for us, And we are glad.'"

REVELATIONS 4:8(NLT)

"Each of these living beings had six wings, and their wings were covered with eyes, inside and out. Day after day and night after night they keep on saying, 'Holy, holy, holy is the Lord God Almighty--the one who always was, who is, and who is still to come.'"

....

....

....

....

....

....

....

....

JUNKIE FIX

WHEN I REALIZE WHAT THE LORD HAS DONE FOR ME I CAN'T HELP BUT PRAISE HIM.

LUKE 21:13(NLT)

"This will be your opportunity to tell them about me."

PHILIPPIANS 1:12(NIV)

"Now I want you to know, brothers, that what has happened to me has really served to advance the gospel. As a result, it has become clear throughout the whole palace guard and to everyone else that I am in chains for Christ. Because of my chains, most of the brothers in the Lord have been encouraged to speak the word of God more courageously and fearlessly."

2THESSALONIANS 1:5(NIV)

"All this is evidence that God's judgment is right, and as a result you will be counted worthy of the kingdom of God, for which you are suffering."

....

....

....

....

....

....

....

....

JUNKIE FIX

....

IN TIMES OF TROUBLE IT IS A PERFECT TIME TO TELL ABOUT GOD IN MY LIFE.

MARK 13:11(NASB)

"When they arrest you and hand you over, do not worry beforehand about what you are to say, but say whatever is given you in that hour; for it is not you who speak, but it is the Holy Spirit."

LUKE 12:12(NLT)

"For the Holy Spirit will teach you what needs to be said even as you are standing there."

LUKE 21:13(NLT)

"This will be your opportunity to tell them about me."

ACTS 4:31(NLT)

"After this prayer, the building where they were meeting shook, and they were all filled with the Holy Spirit. And they preached God's message with boldness."

JUNKIE FIX

WHEN THEY ARREST ME, I HAVE NO NEED TO WORRY. GOD HAS IT HANDLED.

LUKE 12:12(NIV)

"For the Holy Spirit will teach you at that time what you should say."

JOHN 14:26(NKJV)

"But the Helper, the Holy Spirit, whom the Father will send in My name, He will teach you all things, and bring to your remembrance all things that I said to you."

....

....

....

....

....

....

....

....

....

....

....

....

....

....

JUNKIE FIX

IN TIMES OF TROUBLE, THE HOLY SPIRIT COMES TO ME AND WHISPERS WORDS OF WISDOM.

ACTS 3:18(NASB)

"But the things which God announced beforehand by the mouth of all the prophets, that His Christ would suffer, He has thus fulfilled."

PSALM 22:1(NKJV)

"My God, My God, why have You forsaken Me? Why are You so far from helping Me, And from the words of My groaning? O My God, I cry in the daytime, but You do not hear; And in the night season, and am not silent. But You are holy, Enthroned in the praises of Israel. Our fathers trusted in You; They trusted, and You delivered them. They cried to You, and were delivered; They trusted in You, and were not ashamed. But I am a worm, and no man; A reproach of men, and despised by the people. All those who see Me ridicule Me; They shoot out the lip, they shake the head, saying, 'He trusted in the Lord, let Him rescue Him; Let Him deliver Him, since He delights in Him!' But You are He who took Me out of the womb; You made Me trust while on My mother's breasts. I was cast upon You from birth. From My mother's womb You have been My God. Be not far from Me, For trouble is near; For there is none to help. Many bulls have surrounded Me; Strong bulls of Bashan have encircled Me. They gape at Me with their mouths, Like a raging and roaring lion. I am poured out like water, And all My bones are out of joint; My heart is like wax; It has melted within Me. My strength is dried up like a potsherd, And My tongue clings to My jaws; You have brought Me to the dust of death. For dogs have surrounded Me, The congregation of the wicked has enclosed Me. They pierced My hands and

My feet; I can count all My bones. They look and stare at Me. They divide My garments among them, And for My clothing, they cast lots. But You, O Lord, do not be far from Me; O My Strength, hasten to help Me! Deliver Me from the sword, My precious life from the power of the dog. Save Me from the lion's mouth And from the horns of the wild oxen! You have answered Me. I will declare Your name to My brethren; In the midst of the assembly, I will praise You. You, who fear the Lord, praise Him! All you descendants of Jacob, glorify Him, And fear Him, all you offspring of Israel! For He has not despised nor abhorred the affliction of the afflicted; Nor has He hidden His face from Him; But when He cried to Him, He heard. My praise shall be of You in the great assembly; I will pay My vows before those who fear Him. The poor shall eat and be satisfied; Those who seek Him will praise the Lord. Let your heart live forever! All the ends of the world Shall remember and turn to the Lord, And all the families of the nations Shall worship before You. For the kingdom is the Lord's, And He rules over the nations. All the prosperous of the earth Shall eat and worship; All those who go down to the dust Shall bow before Him, Even he who cannot keep himself alive. Posterity shall serve Him. It will be recounted of the Lord to the next generation, They will come and declare His righteousness to a people who will be born, That He has done this."

....

....

....

....

....

Junkie Fix

God Knew the plan from the beginning and He did it anyway because He loves me.

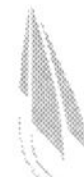

ACTS 4:4(NKJV)

"However, many of those who heard the word believed; and the number of the men came to be about five thousand."

1 THESSALONIANS 1:6(NKJV)

"And you became followers of us and of the Lord, having received the word in much affliction, with joy of the Holy Spirit,"

....

....

....

....

....

....

....

....

....

....

....

....

....

....

JUNKIE FIX

....

THE WORD IS POWERFUL AND LIFE CHANGING. I MUST BE BRAVE TO SHARE IT.

ACTS 4:13(NASB)

"Now as they observed the confidence of Peter and John and understood that they were uneducated and untrained men, they were amazed, and began to recognize them as having been with Jesus."

MATTHEW 11:25(NLT)

"Then Jesus prayed this prayer 'O Father, Lord of heaven and earth, thank you for hiding the truth from those who think themselves so wise and clever, and for revealing it to the childlike.'"

1 CORINTHIANS 1:27(NLT)

"Instead, God deliberately chose things the world considers foolish in order to shame those who think they are wise. And he chose those who are powerless to shame those who are powerful."

....

....

....

....

....

....

....

JUNKIE FIX

....

I CAN BE USED BY GOD. I'M WEAK AND FOOLISH, BUT USEFUL TO HIM.

ACTS 4:17(NLT)

"But perhaps we can stop them from spreading their propaganda. We'll warn them not to speak to anyone in Jesus' name again."

PSALM 119:161(NASB)

"Princes persecute me without cause, But my heart stands in awe of Your words."

DANIEL 6:5(NKJV)

"Then these men said, 'We shall not find any charge against this Daniel unless we find it against him concerning the law of his God.'"

....

....

....

....

....

....

....

....

....

....

JUNKIE FIX

....

I WILL NOT BE SILENCED.

ACTS 4:29(NLT)

"And now, O Lord, hear their threats, and give your servants great boldness in their preaching."

ACTS 4:31(NLT)

"After this prayer, the building where they were meeting shook, and they were all filled with the Holy Spirit. And they preached God's message with boldness."

EPHESIANS 6:19(NIV)

"Pray also for me, that whenever I open my mouth, words may be given me so that I will fearlessly make known the mystery of the gospel,"

JUNKIE FIX

WHEN WAS THE LAST TIME I SPOKE WITH POWER AND AUTHORITY? WHEN WAS THE LAST TIME I WANTED TO?

ACTS 5:20(NIV)

"'Go, stand in the temple courts,' he said, 'and tell the people the full message of this new life.'"

JOHN 11:25(NLT)

"Jesus told her, 'I am the resurrection and the life. Those who believe in me, even though they die like everyone else, will live again. They are given eternal life for believing in me and will never perish. Do you believe this, Martha?'"

....

....

....

....

....

....

....

....

....

....

....

....

....

JUNKIE FIX

....

THE WORDS OF THIS LIFE ARE SO IMPORTANT. WHAT KEEPS ME FROM SHARING THEM?

I find that if I don't challenge myself, I become lazy toward what I have to do. So, this challenge is to share with others the Word and truth of Jesus Christ. The first thing I remember is I am not alone; God helps me say what He wants me to say. This helps when I think of the way Jesus taught others. He was direct, personal, and powerful. With God's help, I can do that. And I have done it many times.

The next part of my challenge is how much I share with others. I can always share more. I wish everyone who knew me would know Christ. It's my calling to share. My self-doubt and care for the relationship I have with my friends stops me sometimes, it is my fear of being alone. I must be brave enough to share the Word. It is powerful and life changing. God provides for all my needs and did not make me to be alone. I worry about nothing, pray about everything. I will not be silenced.

Bible Junkie Hard Core Challenge:

Do

Actions speak louder than I can scream.

ROMANS 6:10(NLT)

"He died once to defeat sin, and now he lives for the glory of God. So, you should consider yourselves dead to sin and able to live for the glory of God through Christ Jesus."

1 PETER 2:24(NLT)

"He personally carried away our sins in his own body on the cross so we can be dead to sin and live for what is right. You have been healed by his wounds!"

JUNKIE FIX

NOTHING ELSE MUST BE DONE. I WAS SICK, NOW I'M HEALED. I CAN LIVE THE WAY JESUS WANTS.

ROMANS 1:12(NKJV)

"That is, that I may be encouraged together with you by the mutual faith both of you and me."

TITUS 1:4(NASB)

"To Titus, my true child in a common faith Grace and peace from God the Father and Christ Jesus our Savior."

JUNKIE FIX

ENCOURAGEMENT IS JUST ONE OF THE GOOD REASONS I MEET TOGETHER WITH CHRISTIANS.

DO

ACTS 28:30(NLT)

"For the next two years, Paul lived in his own rented house. He welcomed all who visited him, proclaiming the Kingdom of God with all boldness and teaching about the Lord Jesus Christ. And no one tried to stop him."

JUNKIE FIX

GOD GIVES US A TIME AND A PLACE TO DO WHAT HE WANTS US TO DO. IT'S NOT FOREVER.

ROMANS 1:8(NIV)

"First, I thank my God through Jesus Christ for all of you, because your faith is being reported all over the world."

ROMANS 16:19(NIV)

"Everyone has heard about your obedience, so I am full of joy over you; but I want you to be wise about what is good, and innocent about what is evil."

JUNKIE FIX

BEING KNOWN AS A FAITHFUL CHRISTIAN IS GREAT. IT IS A BIG RESPONSIBILITY TO KEEP IT UP.

DO

ACTS 21:13(NLT)

"But he said, 'Why all this weeping? You are breaking my heart! For I am ready not only to be jailed at Jerusalem but also to die for the sake of the Lord Jesus.' When it was clear that we couldn't persuade him, we gave up and said, 'The will of the Lord be done.'"

JUNKIE FIX

I HOLD NOTHING BACK FROM LORD JESUS.

ACTS 22:14(NKJV)

DO

"Then he said, 'The God of our fathers has chosen you that you should know His will, and see the Just One, and hear the voice of His mouth. For you will be His witness to all men of what you have seen and heard. And now why are you waiting? Arise and be baptized, and wash away your sins, calling on the name of the Lord.'"

....

....

....

....

....

....

....

....

....

....

....

....

....

....

....

....

JUNKIE FIX

....

WE ALL HAVE A CALLING. THE QUESTION IS ... WHAT ARE WE WAITING FOR?

ACTS 17:2(NKJV)

"Then Paul, as was his custom, went in to them, and for three Sabbaths reasoned with them from the Scriptures,"

ACTS 14:1(NIV)

"At Iconium Paul and Barnabas went as usual into the Jewish synagogue. There they spoke so effectively that a great number of Jews and Gentiles believed."

ACTS 16:13(NIV)

"On the Sabbath we went outside the city gate to the river, where we expected to find a place of prayer. We sat down and began to speak to the women who had gathered there."

....

....

....

....

....

....

....

....

JUNKIE FIX

THE BIBLE DESCRIBES PAUL'S ACTIONS WITH THESE WORDS "AS WAS HIS CUSTOM." ARE MY CUSTOMS POWERFUL? NOBLE? HONORING? GODLY?

ACTS 20:22(NLT)

"And now I am going to Jerusalem, drawn there irresistibly by the Holy Spirit, not knowing what awaits me, except that the Holy Spirit has told me in city after city that jail and suffering lie ahead."

JUNKIE FIX

BE BOLD!

DO

ACTS 13:49(NIV)

"The word of the Lord spread through the whole region. But the Jews incited the God-fearing women of high standing and the leading men of the city. They stirred up persecution against Paul and Barnabas, and expelled them from their region. So they shook the dust from their feet in protest against them and went to Iconium. And the disciples were filled with joy and with the Holy Spirit."

JUNKIE FIX

FOLLOWING GOD'S WORD IS ALWAYS THE BEST, NO MATTER THE OUTCOME.

ACTS 11:28(NASB)

"One of them named Agabus stood up and began to indicate by the Spirit that there would certainly be a great famine all over the world. And this took place in the reign of Claudius. And in the proportion that any of the disciples had means, each of them determined to send a contribution for the relief of the brethren living in Judea."

MATTHEW 25:34(NIV)

"Then the King will say to those on his right, 'Come, you who are blessed by my Father; take your inheritance, the kingdom prepared for you since the creation of the world. For I was hungry and you gave me something to eat, I was thirsty and you gave me something to drink, I was a stranger and you invited me in, I needed clothes and you clothed me, I was sick and you looked after me, I was in prison and you came to visit me.'"

JUNKIE FIX

JUST AS IT SHOULD BE. GOD CALLED. WE ANSWERED!

MARK 1:17(NKJV)

"Then Jesus said to them, 'Follow Me, and I will make you become fishers of men.'"

JUNKIE FIX

NOTHING HAS CHANGED. JESUS CALLED HIS FOLLOWERS AND HE GAVE THEM PURPOSE. HE CALLS ME AND ASKS ME TO OBEY.

LUKE 5:11(NKJV)

"So when they had brought their boats to land, they forsook all and followed Him."

LUKE 9:59(NASB)

"And He said to another, 'Follow Me.' But he said, 'Lord, permit me first to go and bury my father.' But He said to him, 'Allow the dead to bury their own dead; but as for you, go and proclaim everywhere the kingdom of God.' Another also said, 'I will follow You, Lord; but first permit me to say good-bye to those at home.' But Jesus said to him, 'No one, after putting his hand to the plow and looking back, is fit for the kingdom of God.'"

JUNKIE FIX

WHEN GOD CALLS ME, NOTHING ELSE IS IMPORTANT.

LUKE 11:28(NLT)

"He replied, 'But even more blessed are all who hear the word of God and put it into practice.'"

PSALM 1:1(NASB)

"How blessed is the man who does not walk in the counsel of the wicked, Nor stand in the path of sinners, Nor sit in the seat of scoffers! But his delight is in the law of the Lord, And in His law he meditates day and night."

PSALM 119:1(NKJV)

"Blessed are the undefiled in the way, Who walk in the law of the Lord! Blessed are those who keep His testimonies, Who seek Him with the whole heart!'

ISAIAH 48:1(NKJV)

"Thus says the Lord, your Redeemer, The Holy One of Israel ' I am the Lord your God, Who teaches you to profit, Who leads you by the way you should go. Oh, that you had heeded My commandments! Then your peace would have been like a river, And your righteousness like the waves of the sea.'"

MATTHEW 7:21(NLT)

"Not all people who sound religious are really godly. They may refer to me as 'Lord,' but they still won't enter the Kingdom of Heaven. The decisive issue is whether they obey my Father in heaven."

James 1:25(NIV)

"But the man who looks intently into the perfect law that gives freedom, and continues to do this, not forgetting what he has heard, but doing it—he will be blessed in what he does."

Junkie Fix

HEARING GOD'S WORD IS ONLY PART OF HIS BLESSING. DOING GOD'S WILL IS MORE IMPORTANT.

LUKE 11:9(NIV)

"So I say to you Ask and it will be given to you; seek and you will find; knock and the door will be opened to you."

ISAIAH 55:6(NKJV)

"Seek the Lord while He may be found, Call upon Him while He is near."

MATTHEW 21:22(NIV)

"If you believe, you will receive whatever you ask for in prayer."

JOHN 15:7(NIV)

"If you remain in me and my words remain in you, ask whatever you wish, and it will be given you."

JAMES 1:5(NKJV)

"If any of you lacks wisdom, let him ask of God, who gives to all liberally and without reproach, and it will be given to him. But let him ask in faith, with no doubting, for he who doubts is like a wave of the sea driven and tossed by the wind."

....

....

....

....

JUNKIE FIX

IT IS SIMPLE! I BELIEVE JESUS. I SERVE GOD WITH MY LIFE.

PROVERBS 31:8(NKJV)

"Open your mouth for the speechless, In the cause of all who are appointed to die."

JOB 29:15(NLT)

"I served as eyes for the blind and feet for the lame."

PSALM 82:1(NKJV)

"God stands in the congregation of the mighty; He judges among the gods. How long will you judge unjustly, And show partiality to the wicked? Defend the poor and fatherless; Do justice to the afflicted and needy. Deliver the poor and needy; Free them from the hand of the wicked."

JUNKIE FIX

GOD CALLS ME TO ACTION.

ECCLESIASTES 3:10(NKJV)

"I have seen the God-given task with which the sons of men are to be occupied."

....

....

....

....

....

....

....

....

....

....

....

....

....

....

....

....

....

....

....

JUNKIE FIX

....

MY GOD-GIVEN TASK IS TO *FOLLOW GOD.*

MARK 1:15(NLT)

"'At last the time has come!' he announced. 'The Kingdom of God is near! Turn from your sins and believe this Good News!'"

ACTS 20:21(NLT)

"I have had one message for Jews and Gentiles alike--the necessity of turning from sin and turning to God, and of faith in our Lord Jesus."

JUNKIE FIX

IT IS TIME FOR ACTION! REPENT AND BELIEVE!

PROVERBS 1:23(NKJV)

"Turn at my rebuke; Surely I will pour out my spirit on you; I will make my words known to you."

ISAIAH 32:15(NKJV)

"Until the Spirit is poured upon us from on high, And the wilderness becomes a fruitful field, And the fruitful field is counted as a forest."

JOEL 2:28(NASB)

"It will come about after this That I will pour out My Spirit on all mankind; And your sons and daughters will prophesy, Your old men will dream dreams, Your young men will see visions."

JUNKIE FIX

WHEN I REPENT, THE HOLY SPIRIT IS IN ME. UNDERSTANDING COMES.

PROVERBS 21:3(NIV)

"To do what is right and just is more acceptable to the Lord than sacrifice."

1 SAMUEL 15:22(NLT)

"But Samuel replied, 'What is more pleasing to the Lord your burnt offerings and sacrifices or your obedience to his voice? Obedience is far better than sacrifice. Listening to him is much better than offering the fat of rams.'"

ISAIAH 1:15(NLT)

"From now on, when you lift up your hands in prayer, I will refuse to look. Even though you offer many prayers, I will not listen. For your hands are covered with the blood of your innocent victims. Wash yourselves and be clean! Let me no longer see your evil deeds. Give up your wicked ways. Learn to do good. Seek justice. Help the oppressed. Defend the orphan. Fight for the rights of widows."

MICAH 6:8(NIV)

"He has showed you, O man, what is good. And what does the Lord require of you? To act justly and to love mercy and to walk humbly with your God."

DO

JUNKIE FIX

GOD DOES NOT WANT TO HEAR ANOTHER APOLOGY, HE WANTS TO SEE ME LIVING WELL.

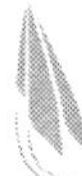

ACTS 20:23(NIV)

"I only know that in every city the Holy Spirit warns me that prison and hardships are facing me. However, I consider my life worth nothing to me, if only I may finish the race and complete the task the Lord Jesus has given me-the task of testifying to the gospel of God's grace."

JUNKIE FIX

I WILL FINISH WHAT GOD TOLD ME TO DO NO MATTER THE COST.

PROVERBS 28:13(NLT)

"People who cover over their sins will not prosper. But if they confess and forsake them, they will receive mercy."

1 JOHN 1:6(NKJV)

"If we say that we have fellowship with Him, and walk in darkness, we lie and do not practice the truth. But if we walk in the light as He is in the light, we have fellowship with one another, and the blood of Jesus Christ His Son cleanses us from all sin. If we say that we have no sin, we deceive ourselves, and the truth is not in us. If we confess our sins, He is faithful and just to forgive us our sins and to cleanse us from all unrighteousness If we say that we have not sinned, we make Him a liar, and His word is not in us."

....

....

....

....

....

....

....

....

JUNKIE FIX

....

TO BE RIGHT WITH GOD, MY SIN CAN NOT BE COVERED. IT MUST BE CONFESSED AND NOT DENIED, TO BE RIGHT WITH GOD.

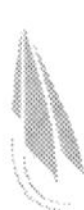

PROVERBS 4:18(NKJV)

"But the path of the just is like the shining sun, That shines ever brighter unto the perfect day."

PHILIPPIANS 2:15(NLT)

"So that no one can speak a word of blame against you. You are to live clean, innocent lives as children of God in a dark world full of crooked and perverse people. Let your lives shine brightly before them.'

JUNKIE FIX

MY GOAL AS A BELIEVER IS TO HAVE MORE OF THE LIGHT OF GOD IN ME. I WANT TO SHINE LIKE THE NOONDAY SUN.

LUKE 10:17(NASB)

"The seventy returned with joy, saying, 'Lord, even the demons are subject to us in Your name.'"

PSALM 91:13(NLT)

"You will trample down lions and poisonous snakes; you will crush fierce lions and serpents under your feet!"

MARK 16:18(NKJV)

"They will take up serpents; and if they drink anything deadly, it will by no means hurt them; they will lay hands on the sick, and they will recover."

LUKE 10:1(NASB)

"Now after this the Lord appointed seventy others, and sent them in pairs ahead of Him to every city and place where He Himself was going to come."

JUNKIE FIX

BEING A SERVANT OF CHRIST, I CAN DO GREAT THINGS IN HIS NAME. HE SHALL PROTECT ME.

LUKE 9:6(NIV)

"So they set out and went from village to village, preaching the gospel and healing people everywhere."

LUKE 8:1(NKJV)

"Now it came to pass, afterward, that He went through every city and village, preaching and bringing the glad tidings of the kingdom of God. And the twelve were with Him."

JUNKIE FIX

DISCIPLES DID EXACTLY AS THEY WERE TOLD, FOLLOWING JESUS.

LUKE 9:2(NKJV)

"He sent them to preach the kingdom of God and to heal the sick."

MATTHEW 10:7(NASB)

"And as you go, preach, saying, 'The kingdom of heaven is at hand. Heal the sick, raise the dead, cleanse the lepers, cast out demons. Freely you received, freely give.'"

MARK 6:12(NIV)

"They went out and preached that people should repent."

....

....

....

....

....

....

....

....

....

....

JUNKIE FIX

....

WHEN GOD CALLS; HE EMPOWERS ME TO DO WHAT HE ASKS.

MARK 13:13(NKJV)

"And you will be hated by all for My name's sake. But he who endures to the end shall be saved."

MATTHEW 24:9(NKJV)

"Then they will deliver you up to tribulation and kill you, and you will be hated by all nations for My name's sake."

REVELATIONS 2:10(NLT)

"Don't be afraid of what you are about to suffer. The Devil will throw some of you into prison and put you to the test. You will be persecuted for `ten days.' Remain faithful even when facing death and I will give you the crown of life."

JUNKIE FIX

I WILL STAND FIRM TO THE END.

LUKE 11:4(NIV)

"Forgive us our sins, for we also forgive everyone who sins against us. And lead us not into temptation."

EPHESIANS 4:32(NLT)

"Instead, be kind to each other, tenderhearted, forgiving one another, just as God through Christ has forgiven you."

JUNKIE FIX

GOD TELLS ME LOVINGLY TO "PLAY NICE WITH OTHERS."

MARK 16:15(NKJV)

"And He said to them, 'Go into all the world and preach the gospel to every creature. He who believes and is baptized will be saved; but he who does not believe will be condemned. And these signs will follow those who believe In My name they will cast out demons; they will speak with new tongues; they will take up serpents; and if they drink anything deadly, it will by no means hurt them; they will lay hands on the sick, and they will recover.'"

LUKE 10:17(NKJV)

"Then the seventy returned with joy, saying, 'Lord, even the demons are subject to us in Your name.'"

LUKE 10:19(NASB)

"Behold, I have given you authority to tread on serpents and scorpions, and over all the power of the enemy, and nothing will injure you."

JOHN 3:36(NASB)

"He who believes in the Son has eternal life; but he who does not obey the Son will not see life, but the wrath of God abides on him."

ACTS 2:4(NIV)

"All of them were filled with the Holy Spirit and began to speak in other tongues as the Spirit enabled them."

ACTS 5:15(NLT)

"As a result of the apostles' work, sick people were brought out into the streets on beds and mats so that Peter's shadow might fall across some of them as he went by. Crowds came in from the villages around Jerusalem, bringing their sick and those possessed by evil spirits, and they were all healed."

ACTS 8:7(NLT)

"Many evil spirits were cast out, screaming as they left their victims. And many who had been paralyzed or lame were healed."

ACTS 19:12(NLT)

"So that even when handkerchiefs or cloths that had touched his skin were placed on sick people, they were healed of their diseases, and any evil spirits within them came out."

ROMANS 10:8(NLT)

"Salvation that comes from trusting Christ--which is the message we preach--is already within easy reach. In fact, the Scriptures say, 'The message is close at hand; it is on your lips and in your heart.' For if you confess with your mouth that Jesus is Lord and believe in your heart that God raised him from the dead, you will be saved. For it is by believing in your heart that you are made right with God, and it is by confessing with your mouth that you are saved."

1 Corinthians 12:10(NET)

"He gives one person the power to perform miracles, and to another the ability to prophesy. He gives someone else the ability to know whether it is really the Spirit of God or another spirit that is speaking. Still another person is given the ability to speak in unknown languages, and another is given the ability to interpret what is being said."

James 5:14(NKJV)

"Is anyone among you sick? Let him call for the elders of the church, and let them pray over him, anointing him with oil in the name of the Lord."

Junkie Fix

When I do works in the Lord's name, He gives me authority and backs me up.

MARK 1:38(NIV)

"Jesus replied, 'Let us go somewhere else—to the nearby villages—so that I can preach there also. That is why I have come.'"

ISAIAH 61:1(NASB)

"The Spirit of the Lord God is upon me, Because the Lord has anointed me To bring good news to the afflicted; He has sent me to bind up the brokenhearted, To proclaim liberty to captives And freedom to prisoners; To proclaim the favorable year of the Lord And the day of vengeance of our God; To comfort all who mourn,"

JOHN 17:8(NKJV)

"For I have given to them the words which You have given Me; and they have received them, and have known surely that I came forth from You; and they have believed that You sent Me."

JUNKIE FIX

GOD'S WORD IS FOR EVERYONE. I MUST TAKE IT TO THEM.

MARK 3:25(NASB)

"If a kingdom is divided against itself, that kingdom cannot stand."

JUNKIE FIX

GOD GIVES GOOD PARENTING ADVICE.

PROVERBS 19:14(NASB)

"House and wealth are an inheritance from fathers, But a prudent wife is from the Lord."

PROVERBS 12:4(NKJV)

"An excellent wife is the crown of her husband, But she who causes shame is like rottenness in his bones."

PROVERBS 18:22(NKJV)

"He who finds a wife finds a good thing, And obtains favor from the Lord."

PROVERBS 31:10(NKJV)

"Who can find a virtuous wife? For her worth is far above rubies. The heart of her husband safely trusts her; So he will have no lack of gain. She does him good and not evil All the days of her life. She seeks wool and flax, And willingly works with her hands. She is like the merchant ships, She brings her food from afar. She also rises while it is yet night, And provides food for her household, And a portion for her maidservants. She considers a field and buys it; From her profits, she plants a vineyard. She girds herself with strength, And strengthens her arms. She perceives that her merchandise is good, And her lamp does not go out by night. She stretches out her hands to the distaff, And her hand holds the spindle. She extends her hand to the poor, Yes, she reaches out her hands to the needy. She is not afraid of snow for her household, For all her household is clothed with scarlet. She makes tapestry for herself; Her clothing is fine linen and purple. Her husband is known in the gates, When

he sits among the elders of the land. She makes linen garments and sells them, And supplies sashes for the merchants. Strength and honor are her clothing; She shall rejoice in time to come. She opens her mouth with wisdom, And on her tongue is the law of kindness. She watches over the ways of her household, And does not eat the bread of idleness. Her children rise up and call her blessed; Her husband also, and he praises her 'Many daughters have done well, But you excel them all.' Charm is deceitful and beauty is passing, But a woman who fears the Lord, she shall be praised. Give her of the fruit of her hands, And let her own works praise her in the gates."

JUNKIE FIX

A GOOD WIFE IS A DIVINE BLESSING.

MARK 8:34(NASB)

"And He summoned the crowd with His disciples, and said to them, 'If anyone wishes to come after Me, he must deny himself, and take up his cross and follow Me.'"

MATTHEW 10:38(NASB)

"And he who does not take his cross and follow after Me is not worthy of Me."

JUNKIE FIX

FOLLOWING CHRIST MEANS THAT I GET IS MORE THAN WHAT I SACRIFICED.

LUKE 1:74(NKJV)

"To grant us that we, being delivered from the hand of our enemies, might serve Him without fear,"

ROMANS 6:18(NLT)

"Now you are free from sin, your old master, and you have become slaves to your new master, righteousness."

JUNKIE FIX

BEING SAVED MEANS NO LONGER FEARING SIN, MAN, OR DEATH. I'M FREE TO SERVE GOD BOLDLY.

PROVERBS 21:21(NKJV)

"He who follows righteousness and mercy finds life, righteousness, and honor."

MATTHEW 5:6(NLT)

"God blesses those who are hungry and thirsty for justice, for they will receive it in full. God blesses those who are merciful, for they will be shown mercy."

MATTHEW 6:33(NKJV)

"But seek first the kingdom of God and His righteousness, and all these things shall be added to you."

ROMANS 2:7(NLT)

"He will give eternal life to those who persist in doing what is good, seeking after the glory and honor and immortality that God offers."

1 CORINTHIANS 15:58(NET)

"So then, dear brothers and sisters, be firm. Do not be moved! Always be outstanding in the work of the Lord, knowing that your labor is not in vain in the Lord."

JUNKIE FIX

WHEN I WORK TO BE RIGHTEOUS AND MERCIFUL, I RECEIVE SO MUCH MORE.

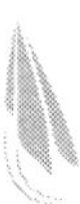

LUKE 21:36(NKJV)

"Watch therefore, and pray always that you may be counted worthy to escape all these things that will come to pass, and to stand before the Son of Man."

PSALM 1:5(NASB)

"Therefore the wicked will not stand in the judgment, Nor sinners in the assembly of the righteous."

MATTHEW 25:13(NKJV)

"Watch therefore, for you know neither the day nor the hour in which the Son of Man is coming."

EPHESIANS 6:13(NIV)

"Therefore put on the full armor of God, so that when the day of evil comes, you may be able to stand your ground, and after you have done everything, to stand."

EPHESIANS 6:18(NLT)

"Pray at all times and on every occasion in the power of the Holy Spirit. Stay alert and be persistent in your prayers for all Christians everywhere."

COLOSSIANS 4:2(NLT)

"Devote yourselves to prayer with an alert mind and a thankful heart."

DO

JUNKIE FIX

PRAY! BE COUNTED AS GOD'S SAVED WHEN HE COMES.

LUKE 14:13(NASB)

"But when you give a reception, invite the poor, the crippled, the lame, the blind, and you will be blessed, since they do not have the means to repay you; for you will be repaid at the 1resurrection of the righteous."

NEHEMIAH 8:10(NASB)

"Then he said to them, 'Go, eat of the fat, drink of the sweet, and send portions to him who has nothing prepared; for this day is holy to our Lord. Do not be grieved, for the joy of the Lord is your strength.'"

MATTHEW 25:35(NKJV)

"For I was hungry and you gave Me food; I was thirsty and you gave Me drink; I was a stranger and you took Me in; I was naked and you clothed Me; I was sick and you visited Me; I was in prison and you came to Me."

MATTHEW 25:40(NKJV)

"And the King will answer and say to them, 'Assuredly, I say to you, inasmuch as you did it to one of the least of these My brethren, you did it to Me.'"

....

....

....

....

JUNKIE FIX

....

GOD ASKS ME TO BE GOOD TO THOSE WHO CANNOT REPAY ME. HE WILL BLESS ME FOR THEM.

LUKE 5:16(NLT)

"But Jesus often withdrew to the wilderness for prayer."

MATTHEW 14:23(NKJV)

"And when He had sent the multitudes away, He went up on the mountain by Himself to pray. Now when evening came, He was alone there."

MARK 1:35(NIV)

"Very early in the morning, while it was still dark, Jesus got up, left the house and went off to a solitary place, where he prayed."

LUKE 6:12(NASB)

"It was at this time that He went off to the mountain to pray, and He spent the whole night in prayer to God."

JUNKIE FIX

PRAYER IS A NEED. IT NEEDS TO BE JUST GOD AND ME ... HOURLY.

LUKE 12:40(NIV)

“You also must be ready, because the Son of Man will come at an hour when you do not expect him.”

MATTHEW 25:13(NKJV)

“Watch therefore, for you know neither the day nor the hour in which the Son of Man is coming.

MARK 13:33(NLT)

“And since you don’t know when they will happen, stay alert and keep watch.”

LUKE 21:34(NLT)

““Watch out! Don’t let me find you living in careless ease and drunkenness, and filled with the worries of this life. Don’t let that day catch you unaware,”

1THESSALONIANS 5:6(NIV)

“So then, let us not be like others, who are asleep, but let us be alert and self-controlled.”

JUNKIE FIX

JESUS IS COMING! DO NOT LOOK FORWARD TO IT BUT BE READY.

DO

LUKE 1:77(NKJV)

"To give knowledge of salvation to His people By the remission of their sins,

JEREMIAH 31:34(NLT)

"And they will not need to teach their neighbors, nor will they need to teach their family, saying, 'You should know the Lord.' For everyone, from the least to the greatest, will already know me,' says the Lord. 'And I will forgive their wickedness and will never again remember their sins.'"

....

....

....

....

....

....

....

....

....

....

....

....

JUNKIE FIX

....

I TEACH WHAT I HAVE LEARNED; CONFESS, REPENT, AND BE SAVED.

ACTS 1:8(NASB)

"But you will receive power when the Holy Spirit has come upon you; and you shall be My witnesses both in Jerusalem, and in all Judea and Samaria, and even to the remotest part of the earth."

ACTS 1:4(NKJV)

"And being assembled together with them, He commanded them not to depart from Jerusalem, but to wait for the Promise of the Father, 'which,' He said, 'you have heard from Me;'"

LUKE 24:49(NASB)

"And behold, I am sending forth the promise of My Father upon you; but you are to stay in the city until you are clothed with power from on high."

....

....

....

....

....

....

....

....

JUNKIE FIX

....

THE LORD SPEAKS TO ME, PROMISES AND EMPOWERMENT. IT IS MY DUTY TO DO, AND TELL WHAT HE ASKS WHEN HE ASKS ME TO DO IT.

ACTS 3:6(NIV)

"Then Peter said, "Silver or gold I do not have, but what I have I give you. In the name of Jesus Christ of Nazareth, walk."

ACTS 4:10(NIV)

"Then know this, you and all the people of Israel
It is by the name of Jesus Christ of Nazareth, whom you crucified but whom God raised from the dead, that this man stands before you healed.

JUNKIE FIX

DON'T HOLD BACK IN PRAYER OR TESTIFYING... BE BOLD!

ACTS 3:12(NLT)

"Peter saw his opportunity and addressed the crowd. 'People of Israel,' he said, 'what is so astounding about this? And why look at us as though we had made this man walk by our own power and godliness?'"

JOHN 5:30(NASB)

"I can do nothing on My own initiative. As I hear, I judge; and My judgment is just, because I do not seek My own will, but the will of Him who sent Me."

ISAIAH 49:3(NASB)

"He said to Me, 'You are My Servant, Israel, In Whom I will show My glory.'"

JUNKIE FIX

I DO MY BEST TO SHOW GOD'S GREATNESS. I HAVE NONE.

ACTS 7:59(NLT)

"And as they stoned him, Stephen prayed, 'Lord Jesus, receive my spirit.' And he fell to his knees, shouting, 'Lord, don't charge them with this sin!' And with that, he died."

MATTHEW 5:44(NKJV)

"But I say to you, love your enemies, bless those who curse you, do good to those who hate you, and pray for those who spitefully use you and persecute you."

JUNKIE FIX

I PRAY THAT I DIE THAT WELL.

ACTS 11:23(NIV)

"When he arrived and saw the evidence of the grace of God, he was glad and encouraged them all to remain true to the Lord with all their hearts. He was a good man, full of the Holy Spirit and faith, and a great number of people were brought to the Lord."

ACTS 13:43(NIV)

"When the congregation was dismissed, many of the Jews and devout converts to Judaism followed Paul and Barnabas, who talked with them and urged them to continue in the grace of God."

JUNKIE FIX

EVERYONE NEEDS ENCOURAGEMENT. FAITHFUL BELIEVERS ARE NO DIFFERENT.

DO

ACTS 4:18(NLT)

"So they called the apostles back in and told them never again to speak or teach about Jesus. But Peter and John replied, 'Do you think God wants us to obey you rather than him?'"

JUNKIE FIX

I DO WHAT GOD TELLS ME.

I can't hold back. God doesn't give me forever to do what I am called to do, I have to do it now. Being saved I no longer fear sin, man, or death. I can serve boldly, and live the way Jesus wants me to. I stand faithful. God is in charge of the results. My job is to share Jesus Christ but I am not held responsible for the belief of every person. I do my best and God blesses the works of my hands.

I encourage everyone to step out in the Lord's calling. You are God's people. Continue in faithful service. Thank you for your work.

FINAL THOUGHTS...

FINAL THOUGHTS...

FINAL THOUGHTS...

FINAL THOUGHTS...

FINAL THOUGHTS...

ABOUT A JUNKIE

My life until my 22nd year was an example of Ecclesiastes 2:11(NASB)

"Thus I considered all my activities which my hands had done and the labor which I had exerted, and behold all was vanity and striving after wind and there was no profit under the sun." Everything I longed for was pointless and left me feeling empty. My soul was in a state of longing. Proverbs 27:20(NKJV) "Hell and Destruction are never full; So the eyes of man are never satisfied." I was consumed by lust, anger, depression, and the only thing that would get my mind off my emptiness was my depravity.

God is incredible and wonderful. He showed this to me. Romans 5:8(NIV)

"But God demonstrates his own love for us in this While we were still sinners, Christ died for us. He gave His life for me while I proved I did not love Him in my sin.

My life was changed when I was humbled. All I had gotten for myself was taken away. I knew that all I did in my own power would fail. I committed all of me to God. I found myself growing and filling with My Lord and Savior. I had a longing to be like Jesus in everyway.

Mercy, truth, wisdom, and understanding began to have importance in my life as I followed Christ's example. I realized the Lord guides, keeps, uses, and loves me. I am still growing and learning, thanks to God's grace.

I believe God has cleansed me of my past to use me for His glory now and in the future. 2 Timothy 2:20,21(NASB)

"Now in a large house there are not only gold and silver vessels, but also vessels of wood and of earthenware, and some to honor and some to dishonor. Therefore, if anyone cleanses himself from these things, he will be a vessel for honor, sanctified, useful to the Master, prepared for every good work."

Since giving my whole life to Him, He has used me for His good works, here and worldwide. He has led me into many places I never would have chosen for myself. I have worked with many lost souls, prodigal children, addicts, prisoners, orphans, and refugees. I never thought I would ever be in a place to help any of these people. I shared with them the love of Christ where they were. God gave me a love for each one. This book is not only an outreach tool but also a thank you letter to God.

God Bless

Lightning Source UK Ltd.
Milton Keynes UK
UKOW05f1014170314

228261UK00001B/4/P